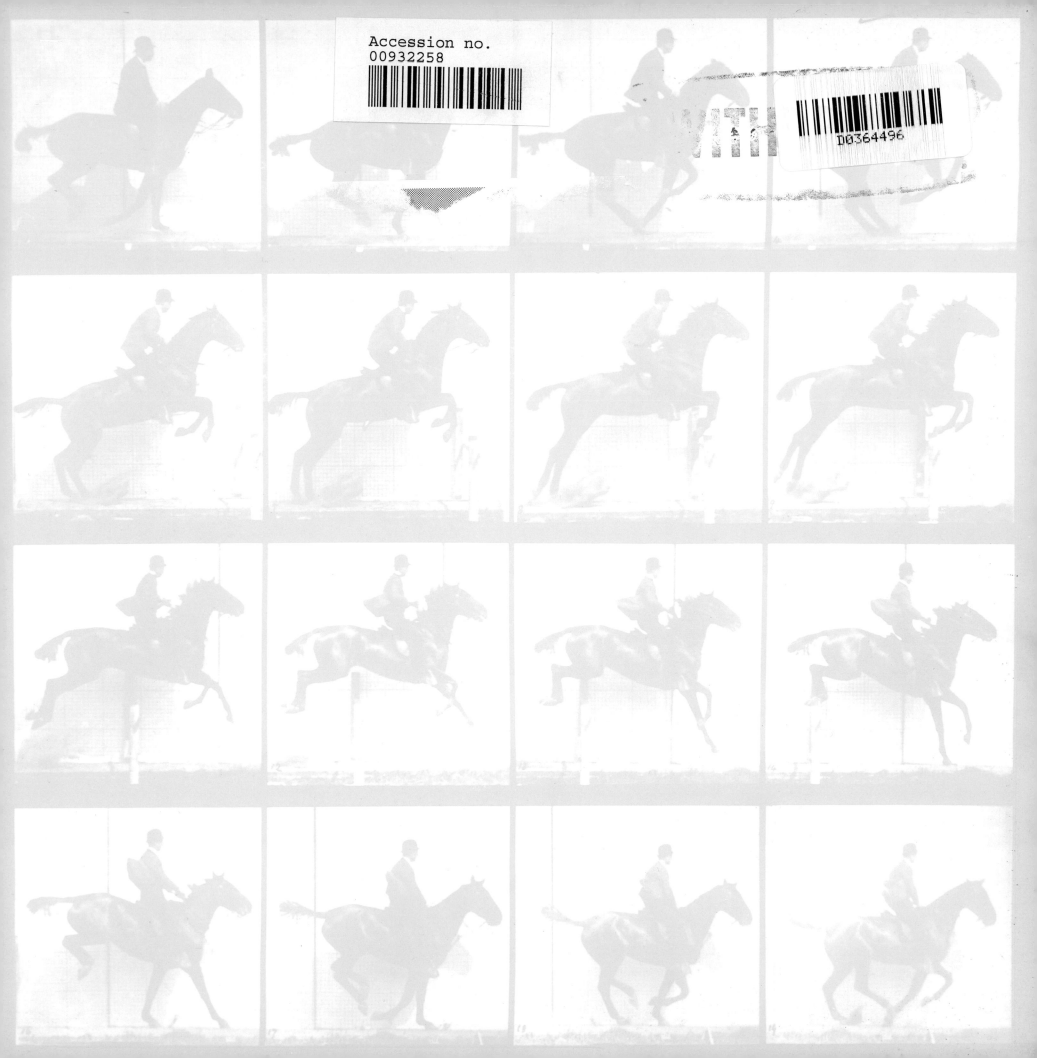

THE HORSE: PHOTOGRAPHIC IMAGES, 1839 TO THE PRESENT

THE HORSE

PHOTOGRAPHIC IMAGES, 1839 TO THE PRESENT

BY GERALD LANG AND LEE MARKS

WITH AN ESSAY BY

ELIZABETH ATWOOD LAWRENCE

HARRY N. ABRAMS, INC., PUBLISHERS, NEW YORK

IN ASSOCIATION WITH

THE PALMER MUSEUM OF ART, PENNSYLVANIA STATE UNIVERSITY

FOR JENNIFER AND JOHN

EDITOR: MARGARET DONOVAN
DESIGNER: STEVEN SCHOENFELDER

FRONTISPIECE: HIRO (YASUHIRO WAKABAYASHI).
Running Horse, Montauk, N.Y., 1955.
SILVER PRINT, 4⅝ × 6½"

LIBRARY OF CONGRESS CATALOGING-IN-PUBLICATION DATA
LANG, GERALD.
THE HORSE : PHOTOGRAPHIC IMAGES, 1839 TO THE PRESENT
BY GERALD LANG AND LEE MARKS ;
WITH AN ESSAY BY ELIZABETH ATWOOD LAWRENCE.
P.   CM.
INCLUDES BIBLIOGRAPHICAL REFERENCES AND INDEX.
ISBN 0–8109–3407–8
1. PHOTOGRAPHY OF HORSES.   2. HORSES—PICTORIAL WORKS.
I. MARKS, LEE. II. LAWRENCE, ELIZABETH ATWOOD. III. TITLE.
TR729.H6L36 1991   779'.32—DC20   91–7573 CIP

COPYRIGHT © 1991 BY GERALD LANG AND LEE MARKS

PUBLISHED IN 1991 BY HARRY N. ABRAMS, INCORPORATED, NEW YORK
A TIMES MIRROR COMPANY
ALL RIGHTS RESERVED. NO PART OF THE CONTENTS OF THIS BOOK MAY BE
REPRODUCED WITHOUT THE WRITTEN PERMISSION OF THE PUBLISHER

PRINTED AND BOUND IN JAPAN

IN ADDITION TO OTHER CREDIT INFORMATION PROVIDED, WE GRATEFULLY
ACKNOWLEDGE THE FOLLOWING COPYRIGHTS AND PERMISSIONS:
FRONTISPIECE, COPYRIGHT © HIRO
PAGE 6, COPYRIGHT © THE ESTATE OF AUGUST SANDER
PLATE 42, COPYRIGHT © 1990 THE ART INSTITUTE OF CHICAGO. ALL RIGHTS RESERVED.
PLATE 51, COPYRIGHT © 1990 THE ART INSTITUTE OF CHICAGO. ALL RIGHTS RESERVED.
PLATE 61, COPYRIGHT © 1990 THE ART INSTITUTE OF CHICAGO. ALL RIGHTS RESERVED.
PLATES 64, 107, COPYRIGHT © HENRI CARTIER-BRESSON/MAGNUM PHOTOS, INC.
PLATE 66, REPRODUCED WITH THE PERMISSION OF ILSE BING
PLATE 68, COPYRIGHT © THE ESTATE OF ROBERT CAPA/MAGNUM PHOTOS, INC.
PLATE 69, COPYRIGHT © 1990 ESTATE OF ANDRÉ KERTÉSZ
PLATE 70, COPYRIGHT © ESTATE OF CAS OORTHUYS
PLATE 71, COPYRIGHT © 1971 APERTURE FOUNDATION, INC., PAUL STRAND ARCHIVE
PLATE 72, COPYRIGHT © ESTATE OF MARTIN MUNKÁCSI
PLATE 74, COPYRIGHT © MARTINE FRANCK/MAGNUM PHOTOS, INC.
PLATES 75, 91, REPRODUCED WITH THE PERMISSION OF
BERENICE ABBOTT/COMMERCE GRAPHICS, LTD., INC.

PLATE 77, REPRODUCED WITH THE PERMISSION OF ESTHER BUBLEY
PLATE 78, COPYRIGHT © 1990 THE ART INSTITUTE OF CHICAGO. ALL RIGHTS RESERVED.
PLATE 79, COPYRIGHT © 1984 IRVING PENN
PLATE 80, COPYRIGHT © 1981 ARIZONA BOARD OF REGENTS,
CENTER FOR CREATIVE PHOTOGRAPHY
PLATE 81, REPRODUCED WITH THE PERMISSION OF THE ESTATE OF WALKER EVANS
PLATE 83, COPYRIGHT © 1981 ARIZONA BOARD OF REGENTS,
CENTER FOR CREATIVE PHOTOGRAPHY
PLATE 84, COPYRIGHT © 1949 ESTATE OF HAROLD E. EDGERTON
PLATES 86, 97, REPRODUCED WITH THE PERMISSION OF JOANNE T. STEICHEN
PLATE 89, COPYRIGHT 1991 ARS, N.Y./A.D.A.G.P.
COURTESY MAN RAY TRUST, PARIS
PLATE 95, REPRINTED WITH THE PERMISSION OF GILBERTE BRASSAÏ
PLATE 96, COPYRIGHT © LEONARD FREED/MAGNUM PHOTOS, INC.
PLATE 98, COURTESY OF THE TRUSTEES OF THE ANSEL ADAMS
PUBLISHING RIGHTS TRUST. ALL RIGHTS RESERVED.
PLATE 99, COPYRIGHT © 1955, APERTURE FOUNDATION, INC., PAUL STRAND ARCHIVE
PLATE 100, REPRODUCED WITH THE PERMISSION OF
THE ESTATE OF BILL BRANDT
PLATE 101, COPYRIGHT © WALTER ROSENBLUM
PLATE 102, COPYRIGHT © 1962, APERTURE FOUNDATION, INC., PAUL STRAND ARCHIVE
PLATE 103, REPRODUCED WITH THE PERMISSION OF ROBERT FRANK
PLATE 104, COPYRIGHT © 1982 THE OAKLAND MUSEUM.
THE CITY OF OAKLAND
PLATE 105, COPYRIGHT © ELLIOTT ERWITT/MAGNUM PHOTOS, INC.
PLATE 106, COPYRIGHT © DENNIS STOCK/MAGNUM PHOTOS, INC.
PLATE 108, COPYRIGHT © EVE ARNOLD/MAGNUM PHOTOS, INC.
PLATE 109, COPYRIGHT © DAVID HURN/MAGNUM PHOTOS, INC.
PLATE 110, COPYRIGHT © RENÉ BURRI/MAGNUM PHOTOS, INC.
PLATE 111, COPYRIGHT © LUCIEN CLERGUE
PLATES 113, 114, COPYRIGHT © JOSEF KOUDELKA/MAGNUM PHOTOS, INC.
PLATES 115, 117, COPYRIGHT © ALEN MACWEENEY
PLATE 116, COPYRIGHT © BRUCE DAVIDSON/MAGNUM PHOTOS, INC.
PLATE 118, COPYRIGHT © 1985 ELIOT PORTER
PLATE 120, COPYRIGHT © O. WINSTON LINK
PLATE 122, COPYRIGHT © DANNY LYON/MAGNUM PHOTOS, INC.
PLATE 125, COPYRIGHT © AARON SISKIND
PLATE 126, COPYRIGHT © 1974 RALPH GIBSON, FROM *DAYS AT SEA*
PLATE 127, COPYRIGHT © THE HEIRS OF W. EUGENE SMITH/BLACK STAR
PLATE 128, COPYRIGHT © LEE FRIEDLANDER
PLATE 131, COPYRIGHT © 1972 ELAINE MAYES
PLATE 132, REPRODUCED WITH THE PERMISSION OF HELEN LEVITT
PLATE 133, COPYRIGHT © 1982 OLIVIA PARKER
PLATE 134, COPYRIGHT © 1988 SALLY MANN
PLATE 137, COPYRIGHT © JED DEVINE
PLATE 143, COPYRIGHT © RICHARD MISRACH
PLATE 140, COPYRIGHT © THE ESTATE OF ANDY WARHOL
PLATE 152, REPRODUCED WITH THE PERMISSION OF RICHARD PRINCE

CONTENTS

AUGUST SANDER. CHILD ON HORSEBACK. C. 1935. SILVER PRINT, 4⅝ × 6⅛"

PEOPLE AND HORSES: AN ENDURING RELATIONSHIP

BY ELIZABETH ATWOOD LAWRENCE

Relationships between people and horses—in their many complex, varied, and multi-dimensional forms—have profoundly affected human life and culture. Indeed, the special bond that exists between the two species has often determined the course of history. Although the earliest use of the horse probably was for food,[1] exploitation of the equine's tremendous potential for supplying power became the hallmark of many early civilizations, and the harnessing of its strength and swiftness to provide mobility transformed human existence. Because of its magnificent contributions to human welfare and enrichment, the horse became inextricably interwoven with the cultural, aesthetic, and spiritual spheres of life as well as with utilitarian purposes. Once the species had established a close relationship of interdependence with people in a horse-centered culture, that society often spurned the meat of its working partners, typically establishing a strong taboo against horseflesh. The horse is undoubtedly the only animal whose consumption by Christians was specifically prohibited by papal decree.[2] Although it is currently an acceptable food in some areas of the world, horsemeat is regarded with disdain, and even horror, by many people.[3]

That horses have been almost universally held in high regard is not difficult to understand, for "learning to control such a remarkable beast was probably the most exciting development in man's history, next to the invention of the wheel."[4] It is generally believed that horses were employed to draw chariots in the ancient world before their widespread use for riding,[5] though some historians disagree. One of the earliest known depictions of a person mounted on a horse is a painted wooden statuette from Egypt, dating to about 2500–1800 B.C.[6]

Evidence indicates that the domestication of horses had definitely taken place by about 3000–2500 B.C.[7] Though it is generally accepted that the horse was not domesticated by Paleolithic or Mesolithic people, certain intriguing discoveries have led some scholars to believe that the animal was being used at a much earlier date. An Ice Age cave painting from France, for example, shows a horse with a line across its head that is strongly suggestive of a harness. Even more convincing is a 14,000- to 15,000-year-old carving of a horse head from a cave site in the Pyrenees that bears engraved lines resembling a halter. Additionally, the finding of horse teeth dating from 30,000 years ago and showing signs of the kind of wear produced only by crib-biting provides another kind of tantalizing archaeological data. Since the repetitive behavior of biting on hard objects, an equine habit often related to the boredom of confinement, is unknown in wild horses and occurs only in animals regularly tethered or stabled for considerable periods of time, the implication of such evidence is that horses were already at least tamed and controlled by Ice Age people.[8]

It is definitely known that relatively early in human history certain societies arose whose chief distinguishing characteristic was the centrality of the horse. The celebrated nomadic equestrian people, the Mongols, conquered one of the most extensive empires in history, largely through their skillful use of cavalry. Every Mongol warrior formed a close, intercommunicating unit with his superbly trained mount. Marco Polo wrote that Mongol riders could remain mounted for days at a time, eating and sleeping on horseback.[9] (They were able to live on mare's milk supplemented by blood drawn from the veins of their horses.) Though they became legendary as barbaric and merciless enemies in war, the Mongols generally treated their horses with care and devotion.[10]

Virtually all mounted societies, from the beginning, established a reputation for being fierce and imperious. On a practical level, of course, the animals did give their riders an over-whelming military advantage against pedestrian peoples; the mobility and power accruing from the mounted state were exploited to assure victory for those who possessed horses. The superiority bestowed upon riders, however, was not only measured in palpable gain, for the psyche of equestrian peoples was deeply affected as well. Living intimately with the equine animal, caring for it, depending upon it for their way of life and their very existence, yet at the same time controlling it, exerting their will over it, and incorporating its power as a physical extension of their bodies, produced marked effects upon their minds. Thus in mounted societies people not only merged physically with the horses that transported them, they intertwined their fate with the animals as well. Often they projected their sense of self into the relationship, establishing a strong feeling of identification with their mounts.

Unfortunately, an account of the effects upon humankind of riding the first horses—events that from archaeological evidence probably took place somewhere in the Ukrainian steppes—is lost to history. But horse peoples, from the Scythians and Assyrians of the ancient world, to the Cossacks of Russia, the gauchos of Argentina, and the cowboys of the American frontier, have generally been characterized as bold, fearless, aggressive, proud, and defiant. The experience of the North American Plains Indians as equestrians not only illustrates the swiftness with which the horse, once acquired by a people, can be completely incorporated into a society, but it also shows the transforming effects of the animal upon the adapting culture. Several decades after becoming mounted, these nomadic tribes could rightly be called the "Lords of the Plains": their ferocity and daring as warriors on horseback made them a scourge to their enemies. As early as 1803, the fur trader Alexander Henry noted the effect of the introduction of the horse upon the Indians and complained that though horses "are useful animals," their acquisition had made the natives "indolent and insolent."[11]

Horses confer a feeling of heightened self-worth that is reflected in the behavior and perceptions of the people who interact with them. And throughout much of human social history, it has been the rule that horses, both in a literal and symbolic sense, elevate the status of those who ride and use them. As historian Walter Prescott Webb wrote, "The horse has always exerted a peculiar emotional effect on both the rider and the observer: he has raised the rider above himself, has increased his power and sense of power, and has aroused a sense of inferiority and envy in the humble pedestrian. . . . Through long ages the horse has been the symbol of superiority, of victory and triumph." He goes on to quote Lord Herbert: "A good rider on a good horse is as much above himself and others as the world can make him."[12]

Its role in raising humankind to an exalted state, in addition to the many material benefits it alone provided prior to the machine age, earned considerable esteem for the horse in most societies. Equestrians are, literally and figuratively, "looked up to." Pride and arrogance often go with the mounted state; contemporary usage perpetuates the linkage, as in the warning to the haughty, "Get off your high horse!" From earliest times, there has been a strong association between horses and aristocracy, both in actuality and in symbol. If being astride a horse makes one feel like royalty, all the more reason that kings, princes, and lords must ride, while serfs and peasants walk. Throughout history the ruling elite has frequently reserved horse riding for itself alone. One thinks of Isak Dinesen's unforgettable story of the native African servant, beaten so severely he was said to have willed himself to die, whose crime was riding on his master's horse when ordered to walk.[13]

A historical survey of the world's horse-owning cultures reveals a pervasive theme of high regard for the horse, which is almost universally recognized as the aristocrat among domestic animals and often identified with luxury, leisure, and power.[14] Evidence shows that, beginning with the earliest civilizations, human relationships with horses were especially meaningful. For example, elaborate burials in which as many as twenty-nine horses were arranged in the grave around the body of their master give testament to the bond with the animals experienced by the Scythians, who flourished in the fifth and fourth centuries B.C.[15] And an ancient Mesopotamian fable allows the horse itself to express the esteem in which it is held by society. Speaking to its friend the ox, the horse boasts of "his pleasant life, how he is lodged near the King and great men, how choice and varied his food is and that his flesh is not eaten."[16] Chiv-

alry, embracing a complex of traits that represented ideal behavior for medieval noblemen, derives its name from the French word meaning horse, and knights were paragons of equestrian skill. Historically, the cavalry has been the most aristocratic of the world's military units. The prestige that society grants to the horse persists into modern times; the aura of equine grandeur remains to grace the machine age.

The fact that there may be more horses in America now, when their use is almost entirely restricted to pleasure, than there were during the age when they provided transportation expresses the appreciation that the present society has for horses. Interestingly, the old aristocratic association with horses is symbolically preserved in the formality and the cultural status of many contemporary equine events. The fox hunt, for example, is a carefully perpetuated social ritual requiring strict adherence to prescribed behavior and clothing as well as mode of equitation. Horse shows are events often staged with the highest of elegance, in which black riding habits and top hats set the tone for the exhibitors of magnificent saddle and harness horses. In racing, much personal status and prestige accrue to a victorious horse's owner, who shares in the animal's elevated rank as a Thoroughbred that has proved its superiority by defeating its rivals in "the sport of kings."

My recent field research with urban mounted police revealed that this law-enforcement unit is often viewed as "elitist," both by the officers themselves and by the public. "A policeman on a horse is ten feet tall," officers say, and this position brings special advantages. "Our unit is held in respect because the horse is a majestic animal." Often, in the media, mounted policemen are given a heroic image as "Blue Knights." These "mounties" claim that foot and motorcycle policemen, who refer to them as "prima donnas and glory seekers," envy and resent the special privilege they enjoy and the admiration they receive from people on the street.[17]

Of course, the ownership and use of pleasure horses in the United States today are not restricted to higher social and economic classes or to those who consciously strive for upward mobility. But people who ride and handle horses certainly seem to add to their self-image in a way that brings them a perceived elevation in status within their own particular social order. In addition to the satisfactions horses bring to the present, they symbolize a dual heritage from the past that is associated with prestige. One influential component of American culture, especially in the East and South, is the old concept originating from British and northern European roots that still identifies the horse with the leisured landed aristocracy.[18] Undoubtedly of considerably greater importance in the American consciousness is the more recent and pervasive egalitarian tradition of the Old West, represented by the cowboy as a New World horseman without noble lineage.

For many people, the mounted cowboy-herder continues to embody a longing for a life of freedom, equal opportunity, autonomy, rugged individualism, adventure, and personal fulfillment in the less complex world of the vanished frontier.[19] As the cowboy's companion and essential partner, the horse becomes for modern riders a means to recapture some of the cattle herder's glory. To reject the constraints of mechanized society and ride free over the plains in the wake of the cowboy hero represents a way to recreate an experience of permanent cultural value. Although American pioneer philosophy left no room for rank emanating from aristocratic ancestry, it is ironic that cowboys soon set up their own standards to elevate themselves over and disparage those excluded from their group. Actually classed as "hired hands," cowboys nevertheless developed an imperious attitude that made them sometimes viewed as "the only reigning American royalty."[20] As one cowboy described his fellow cowpunchers, they "set themselves way up above other people who the chances are were no more common and uneducated than themselves."[21]

Horses are powerful symbols worldwide, and whenever they have become significant in human society, people have typically taken inordinate pride in projecting the proper dignified image of themselves as equestrians. Simple transportation has seldom been the only issue involved. If pure expediency were the determining factor, for example, certain African populations would have ridden quaggas instead of horses. Until the 1840s, the quagga, a species of equid, was common in south and central Africa. It was docile, easily tamed and trained for riding, sturdy, and well adapted to its environment. Moreover, quaggas were plentiful and readily available, in contrast to costly foreign horses, which had to be imported by sea. Instead of being used for riding, however, quaggas were hunted to extinction. The English and Boer farmers viewed quaggas more as vermin than as potential mounts, and their self-image did not allow for the riding of an animal that was classified as wild and whose coarse appearance offended their aesthetic taste. Motivated largely by a deeply inculcated belief that only horses of established domesticated breeds represented status, the colonists resisted the obvious utilitarian advantages of using quaggas as riding mounts and chose instead to import horses.[22]

Horses often serve to fulfill nostalgic yearnings for the less complicated life of past eras. Their rhythmic motion has always fascinated humankind and continues to do so more than ever in this mechanized age. Now that the practical need for horse transportation is virtually nonexistent, people ride by choice, not necessity. Present-day cowhands are still known to perform willingly any ranch task if they "can do it horseback," even when there are alternatives. A study of nineteenth-century German immigrants to Brazil who adopted the equestrian way of life soon after arrival in their new land revealed that they were very quickly transformed into people who "do not like to go afoot. Sometimes they lose half an hour or so with the rounding up of their horses in order to make a five minutes' trip to the neighbor's house."[23]

The number of people who ride for sheer pleasure is steadily increasing, but even those who do not ride share in appreciation of the special kinetic qualities of the horse. People find equine motion a source of delight and are often fascinated by analysis of the way a horse places its feet on the ground. Anthropologist A. L. Kroeber wrote of the "flying gallop"—a way of depicting a horse running with full extension of its legs, which was characteristic of many societies and cultures—as wholly symbolic, "used in art because of its suggestion of great speed."[24] Although horses cannot actually run in this position, it was only when the camera proved this fact that artists began to portray horses running in a realistic manner. Until that time, only the African Bushmen's keen eyes enabled them to depict galloping animals with their legs appearing as they actually move.[25] With the photographic work of Eadweard Muybridge, whose book *Animals in Motion* (1957) was first published in

1887 under the title *Animal Locomotion*, and with the analysis of J. D. B. Stillman, who produced *The Horse in Motion* (1882), every detail of the horse's movements at all gaits and in all types of use came under scrutiny.

Motion is a quintessential element of the bond between humans and horses. Horse races reward the swiftest runners with the accolades of society. Hunters and jumpers take hurdles according to a rigid set of standards and patterns. In rodeo bronc-riding contests, there is an opposition between rider and mount—a man-beast antagonism structured into the sport— yet at the same time there is an effort to attain harmony, as the contestant gears his body rhythm to that of the wildly bucking mount. Circus horses perform complex dance routines, and dressage horses demonstrate intricate maneuvers that are the result of arduous training. During all these feats, equestrians are in tune with their horses' rhythmic movement through space. There is a kinetic interaction between equine and human bodies as well as a merging of wills through reciprocal communication channels.

Countless informants interviewed during my field research on urban horses describe the sense of comfort and well-being they experience upon hearing equine hoofbeats. City dwellers say they feel protected and safe to a much greater degree when they hear the clippety-clop of the mounted policemen's horses than when they simply know there is a motorcycle officer or police cruiser nearby. People often express the idea that the rhythmic sounds remind them of the past, and many relate their sense of reassurance to the slower pace of life represented by the equine animal. The gait of the horse is a welcome, natural rhythm in contrast to the tempo of the machinery in the modern, motorized world. The beat recalls an earlier time when human existence was more in harmony with the living environment.[26]

Because of the rhythmicity of their movements, horses are intimately related to people's sense of the passage of time. One of their most persistent symbolic roles has been as the steeds that draw the chariot of the sun across the sky, enabling each day to come and go in a predictable cycle.[27] Ronald Blythe, whose portrait of rural society in Akenfield often centers on the changes in people's lives that came with mechanization, artic-

ulates the horse's role in demarcating time. "Nothing has contributed more to the swift destruction of the old pattern of life in Suffolk than the death of the horse. It carried away with it a quite different perception of time."[28] Historian and expert horseman J. Frank Dobie observed that "the more machinery man gets, the more machined he is. When the traveler got off the horse and into a machine, the tempo of his mind as well as of his locomotion was changed."[29] Anthropologist E. T. Hall described his own sense of time being affected by a horseback journey in which he was "in the grip of nature." He revealed that, after a few days of adjusting to the rhythm of the horse's gait, "I became part of the country again and my whole psyche changed." "The urban tempo," he pointed out, is "out of sync with the body."[30]

The contemporary media sometimes make use of this symbolic association of horses with the passage of time. For example, a popular television advertisement for Budweiser beer shows a horse dramatically in motion across the open landscape while a voice explains the great amount of time the company takes in order to brew beer of the finest quality. The advertising sequence, still centering on the rhythmic movements of the horse, ends with the assertion that because of the slow aging process used in its brewing, Budweiser is the best beer to drink—"time, after time, after time."

The marking out of time is "one of the fundamental applications of order, for no communal human activity can take place without it."[31] Binding a group of people together as a society, it makes possible their participation in shared activities. Thus, in their association with time, horses can represent the social order itself. They participate in parades, which generally celebrate the seasons or commemorate historical events. Whenever tradition is to be invoked for an important event in society, a slow pace with measured tread is imposed to denote solemnity and formality. Thus horses often act as mounts for honor guards or escorts for visiting dignitaries, and their presence at special civic and national occasions like military funerals lends a solemn air of formality not provided by machinery. In such modern ceremonial and state functions, horses represent the historic past, providing the sanction of culture and tradition by symbolizing the social order.[32]

Horses are often said to stand for war and conquest. This connotation is easy to understand, since they were the chief instruments of battle throughout such a large segment of recorded history; many cavalries were officially abolished only as recently as the 1940s. That a large, gentle herbivore whose natural reaction to danger is swift flight can be made to gallop forward into the noise and confusion of a battlefield is a testament to equine obedience to the human will. Herd instinct and adherence to equine social dominance orders play a part in the cavalry charge.[33] The rider in a sense takes the place of the horse's fellow equines, and thus conditioning and human mastery are superimposed upon the animals.[34]

The horse's relevance as a metaphor for man's conquering force rests on the knowledge that this animal upon which the victorious warrior rides has itself been previously conquered, "broken" and trained to make it suitable for human use. The transformation from wild to tame must be reenacted each time an equine becomes a person's working partner. The inherent wildness of horses is a symbolic concept common to daily life, and the species is known to have been more resistant to taming than many other domesticated animals.[35] "It requires no mean skill on the part of man to assert his dominance over such an animal [a wild horse] and break it in for riding."[36] And such domination over the animal metaphorically sets the stage for further conquest. Bucephalus, the spirited war-horse ridden by Alexander the Great, had defied the mastery of all the experts in the kingdom of Macedonia before the youth tamed him. It was Alexander alone who could conquer Bucephalus through overcoming the animal's fears, thus making him a fitting partner for some of the greatest feats of worldly conquest known to history.[37]

Intimate human-horse relationships were often forged in battle. It is difficult to separate the warrior image of General Robert E. Lee from that of his faithful mount, Traveller. The poet Stephen Vincent Benet describes them both as "iron gray," noting that "He and his horse are matches for the strong/Grace of proportion that inhabits both."[38] The flamboyant General George Armstrong Custer received much acclaim as a superb horseman and bold cavalryman during the Civil War and the Indian campaigns. After his death at the Battle of the Little Big Horn in 1876, however, it was the mount of one of his officers,

Captain Myles W. Keogh, who earned worldwide fame for his legendary role as the "only survivor" of Custer's Last Stand. After the rescue of Keogh's mount, Comanche, from the battlefield, the wounded horse was nursed back to health and became the object of a unique set of army orders that not only established his retirement but also his status as an American hero. Enjoying a long life as a much-beloved celebrity, Comanche was a surrogate for the grief of the young nation, which had suffered such an unexpected defeat and loss of life at the hands of the Indians during the year of its centennial celebration. A contemporary parallel illustrating the honor and acclaim given to wounded war mounts involves Sefton, the British Household Cavalry horse severely injured in an Irish Republican Army attack in 1982. The horse's recovery became the focus of worldwide as well as British attention, emphasizing the continued relevance of the strong affective bond between people and horses. According to media coverage of the event and its aftermath, the public expressed sympathy for and identification with the wounded horse to an even greater extent than with the human victims of the bombing.[39]

Numerous instances of war-horses' loyalty to their riders have been recorded. Typical of these is an entry from the 1794 campaign diary of a British cavalryman describing a horse who stayed by his master's dead body for two days before being found by the man's comrades. When the rider was buried where he had fallen, the "faithful animal seemed to show great reluctance to come away without his master, frequently turning his head and neighing, as if wishing his dead master to come and mount him."[40] Elizabeth Custer, writing of her cavalry experiences on the American frontier, recounted harsh and difficult conditions that were ameliorated by the actions of her husband's horse, Dandy, when the general was "met by the dancing motion of a pair of nimble heels, and the softest, most affectionate eyes, while the head turned to rub itself against the arm or shoulder of one the animal loved."[41] Much earlier in history, this archetypal bonding of steeds to warriors found timeless and dramatic expression in Homer's *Iliad*. The Greek epic relates that Achilles had lent his two fine horses to his friend Patroclus to draw his chariot on the Trojan battlefield. When Patroclus was killed, the horses were deeply grieved by the loss of their beloved driver. Weeping, they stood in front of the chariot with their heads bowed to the earth; their soiled manes trailed the ground, and in their sorrow they refused to move.[42]

Human interaction with horses, of course, has its dark side. Instances abound in which the debt society owes to the horse has not been fairly paid. Cavalry mounts who once served their country valiantly have been abandoned in foreign lands, where they have become the objects of exploitation involving extreme brutality.[43] Owen Wister's firsthand account of a horseback trek in the frontier West revealed an example of unspeakable atrocity perpetrated by a rider who, unable to satisfy his anger by merely beating his disobedient horse, gouged out the eye of the animal.[44] Cart horses, drawing human burdens throughout the ages, have been frequent victims of savage cruelty. Though coach horses are now obsolete, their abused and malnourished modern counterparts in some cities still draw vehicles to artificially recreate the past for the amusement of tourists. And society must bear the guilt for such current realities as the drugging of racehorses and the torture inflicted to produce artificial gaits in certain breeds.

Horses—with their sensitivity, innocence, and unusual willingness to give themselves fully to the tasks society demands of them—seem particularly vulnerable to human neglect and cruelty. History is replete with examples of cultures that have practiced animal sacrifice to appease their gods, and the high value assigned to horses has made them prime subjects for ritual bloodshed. In *Equus*, the main character perceives horses as interchangeable with the crucified Christ, and blinding the animals, as he does in the play, becomes the ultimate act of violence toward a sacrificial victim.[45] Barbarity toward the powerful yet submissive equine animal is often peculiarly expressive of human malice. Guy de Maupassant's story of Coco, an old and faithful workhorse who is systematically beaten and starved to death by a vicious youth, is a classic representation of sadism.[46] The theme of a suffering horse often serves in literature as a metaphor for the trials of human beings, the two becoming linked as victims of the same inequitable social system. Tolstoy immortalized the commonality of pain and travail between horses and people in his story of the horse Strider.[47] When this tale was produced as a play in 1980, a man wearing a horse collar and bridle took the part of Strider, and a musical solo sung during the drama reiterated the theme

"Oh, hard is life for man and horse."[48]

The arduous labor of horses was the power that gave rise to nations. When the Spanish conquistadors met with success against their pedestrian foes in their military expeditions to the New World, they acknowledged that "after God, we owed victory to our horses."[49] It was the horse that enabled the United States to grow into the vast country that it became. Several years ago, four distinctly American breeds were honored on commemorative postage stamps because horses were "so instrumental in the development, exploration, and expansion of our nation."[50] Fulfillment of Manifest Destiny required that people be mounted, for the horse was the essential instrument by which both conquest of the wilderness and settlement were made possible. As Owen Wister has asserted, it was not just the American pioneers' special traits that determined the course of history on the American continent, but also the "destiny" that brought the Anglo-Saxon colonists into partnership with a particular kind of horse, the mustang, as their "foster brother" and "ally."[51]

Mustangs are considered to be descendants of the domesticated mounts that were brought to the New World by the Spanish and have since reverted to the feral state. Today, some mustang herds still run free in certain areas of Western rangeland, but their continued existence is called into question because of sharp disagreements concerning their value and significance. Those who want them removed from the range say that the mustangs serve no practical purpose but instead compete with cattle and domestic horses for grass and water and use land that should be reserved for wildlife (especially the game species exploited by hunters). Since the horses are feral and not native wild animals, their detractors claim that they upset the natural balance of the ecosystem. Their defenders look upon American wild horses as living symbols of the historic and pioneer spirit of the West, as an aesthetically vital and cherished part of the nation's heritage. They point out that even though native horses became extinct in North America as a result of some undetermined cause operating just after the last Ice Age, they had previously evolved as a species on the continent and therefore are still ecologically compatible, posing no real threat to indigenous wildlife. Thus the equine animal is today the focus for conflicting American societal value-systems applied to humankind and nature—the economic versus the aesthetic, the pragmatic versus the affective, the tame versus the wild, and the anthropocentric ethos versus the belief in the intrinsic right of all forms of life to survival.

The term most universally and frequently applied to horses is "noble." Somehow the horse's perceived traits—dignity and refinement, grace, beauty, and power—are felt to be transmitted to its human associates. And people of horse-owning societies are prone to take not only their individual self-image but also their ethnic identity from the horses who so typically become the focus of their cultural life. For example, once horses were acquired by the North American Plains Indians and incorporated into tribal culture, they quickly transformed the Indian way of life and became the standard measurement for all that the society held of value. A tribesman with few horses was a pauper who "trudged afoot."[52] The Indians' prowess in horsemanship became legendary, and their partnership with the powerful new animal became one of the closest relationships of interdependence between humankind and animals known to history. Data from my field research indicate that contemporary Plains natives living on the Crow Reservation in Montana continue to identify with this heritage and claim that to be on horseback makes them feel truly Indian. They still find in their horses a distillation of the qualities that are most meaningful in their culture. The animals are instrumental in helping Crow people to define themselves as a social entity and to retain an important part of their own tradition despite encroachment by the dominant society.[53]

Contemporary Crow Indians often compare themselves to the Arabs, who also consider their horses family, and they often express the idea that love for horses flows in both Crow and Arabic blood. In Arabian culture, "horses are riches, joys, life, and religion." Arabs have a sacred duty to give horses good care and are charged for the love of God not to be negligent toward them, lest they "regret it in this life and the next." According to the Prophet, God created the peerless Arabian horse from the wind, and told it, "I have hung happiness from the forelock which hangs between your eyes; you shall be the lord of the other animals. Men shall follow you wherever you go. . . . You shall fly without wings; riches shall be on your back and fortune shall come through your mediation."[54]

In other societies, too, dependence on the horse has led to an attitude of appreciation in which identity became invested in the animal. Traditional Gypsies, for example, feel that the nomadic existence made possible by the horses who draw their caravans is the only way of living worthy of humans.[55] For them, "Life revolves around the horse," and the greeting between friends is not "I hope you will live happily," but rather "May your horses live long."[56] The exalted value given to horses is expressed by the maxim "Gypsy gold does not chink and glitter. It gleams in the sun and neighs in the dark."[57] The belief that "a Gypsy without a horse is no genuine Gypsy"[58] indicates the extent to which the animal has gone beyond utility to become essential to group identity. To Gypsies, horses not only represent the sense of self but also embody intense social meaning. The horse is central to their life-style in that it enables them to move from place to place as their culture dictates. Traditional nomadism sets these people apart both physically and ideologically from the constraints of sedentary living, which they abhor. Their disdain for settled peasants and farmers compares with that of American range cowboys for agriculturalists and other people whose labors make them pedestrians; the cowboys assert that "a man afoot is no man at all."

For those who ride, there is innocence in the horse's nature, a quality enhanced by the paradox of its great strength combined with tractability. The horseman's expression that a certain animal has a "kind eye" articulates this feeling for a creature of enormous power in whom such benevolence toward people can still be found. Horse sense is a highly regarded quality, and stories of equine sagacity commonly feature faithful and heroic horses who serve their masters. Jonathan Swift in *Gulliver's Travels* described horses in his native England as "the most generous and comely animals we had."[59] It was the equine species that Swift chose in depicting the harmonious land of the Houyhnhnms, paragons of rationality, wisdom, and nobility who contrasted so sharply with the Yahoos, human beings of consummately illogical behavior, vices, follies, and degradations. Similarly, for the artist George Stubbs, one of the most skillful and celebrated painters of equine subjects, "The horse was his chief image of social harmony: order on four legs."[60] The dependability of the equine's gentle character—its obedience, mildness, and nonaggression—has been used metaphorically to represent the natural order of the world. In *Macbeth*, for example, Shakespeare employs the image of tame horses, sedate and disciplined herbivores, suddenly going wild and devouring each other's flesh.[61] This frightful transformation dramatizes the enormity of the crime of murder, which not only breaks the human social code but disturbs the very order of nature itself.

Symbolically as well as physically, horses transport people to new places, bearing them out of the mundane realm into the richer sphere of imagination. From childhood, mounts provide the joy of motion, as rocking horses and carousel steeds take us on enchanted journeys. The hobbyhorse, in fact, gives its name to any absorbing interest that metaphorically carries a person away from a humdrum existence. Pegasus, the horse with wings, symbolizes the poetic inspiration that surpasses pragmatic considerations and transcends earthly roots. In certain societies, shamans use symbolic horses that carry them on mystical journeys into the sacred domain, where they can be empowered for curing.[62]

In modern society, too, the horse can play a vital role in healing. As a companion who shares our leisure, it provides exercise, diversion, adventure, beauty and grace, and a sense of communion with nature that returns us to our roots and restores us to a sense of harmony. It is often patient and kind, with a judicious sense of the character of its rider, for a horse is willing to modify its behavior for the young or the handicapped. Therapeutic horseback-riding programs are currently proving to be of inestimable value in promoting the physical and mental health of disabled people. An old adage states that "the best thing for the inside of a person is the outside of a horse," and widely believed folklore holds that association with horses leads to longevity. Mechanization still has not removed from the human consciousness the concept of measuring physical force by "horsepower," and somehow the utility of machines has never really supplanted horses.

Horses are companions of a different order than most other domestic species. Equestrians, like centaurs of old, can merge their own being with the rhythm and power of their mounts, bonding with them in a participatory rather than a passive way, reconfirming the human status as part of the natural world.

The fine-tuned communication between rider and horse is both physical and mental, as the beauty and grace of the horse's movement become qualities possessed by the rider.

Even for people who do not ride, horses represent freedom, power, and romantic beauty. Equines are often likened to the sea, with its rhythmic waves and tides, its surging power, and the vastness that connotes wildness and lack of restraint. As the motion and sounds of the ocean calm and reassure us, relating us to the cosmic cycle, so do our magnificent steeds. Many legends tell of horses originating from the sea, and people from diverse cultures share the idea of an affinity between horses and water. Frequently, too, myths and tales express the concept that horses were born from the wind, the swift element that is the equine animal's only rival in speed of flight. From the wind, horses are perceived to derive their dual capacity for being quiet and docile as a summer breeze or wild and powerful as a winter tempest. As "fiery steeds," horses are also compared with flames and with the sun. Sea, wind, and fire—such similes drawn from nature ultimately associate the horse with the life-giving rhythmicity of the earth.

In the horse's close alliance with people, its complex nature and diverse attributes have enabled the animal to become far more than a worker and helper, vehicle of transport, or tool for sport. The potential for dynamic interaction between people and horses first arose from the social nature of both species and has fostered the development of a unique complementariness. From the beginning of contact between horses and people, the particular qualities that this richly symbolic animal has assumed in the human mind have deepened the relationship, infusing it with mental and spiritual dimensions that have carried the animal far beyond utilitarian considerations.

The horse's capacity to exert a transforming influence upon human beings empowers it as an enduring force in contemporary life. In the present ecological crisis, with the growing awareness of the necessity to reestablish a more harmonious relationship with nature, the age-old question of the human status with regard to the animals with whom we share the earth has taken on new urgency. In articulating this dilemma, the horse—as humankind's ancient servant but also as an ally and friend—is symbolic of the range of interrelationships that bind people to the natural world.

NOTES

1. Juliet Clutton-Brock, *Domesticated Animals From Early Times* (Austin: University of Texas Press, 1981), p. 80.

2. Marvin Harris, *Good to Eat: Riddles of Food and Culture* (New York: Simon & Schuster, 1985), pp. 96–97.

3. Marshall Sahlins, *Culture and Practical Reason* (Chicago: University of Chicago Press, 1976), pp. 172–75.

4. C. E. G. Hope and G. N. Jackson, eds., *The Encyclopedia of the Horse* (London: Peerage Books, 1973), p. 236.

5. Frederick E. Zeuner, *A History of Domesticated Animals* (New York: Harper & Row, 1963), p. 337.

6. Brian Vesey-Fitzgerald, ed., *The Book of the Horse* (Los Angeles: Borden, 1947), p. 26.

7. Zeuner, *History of Domesticated Animals*, p. 337.

8. Richard E. Leakey, *The Making of Mankind* (New York: E. P. Dutton, 1981), pp. 193–96.

9. Luigi Gianoli, *Horses and Horsemanship Through the Ages* (New York: Crown, 1969), p. 71.

10. Michael Seth-Smith, ed., *The Horse in Art and History* (New York: Mayflower Books, 1978), p. 16.

11. Elliott Coues, ed., *New Light on the Early History of the Greater Northwest: The Manuscript Journals of Alexander Henry and David Thompson, 1799–1814*, 3 vols. (New York: Francis P. Harper, 1897), vol. I, p. 225.

12. Walter Prescott Webb, *The Great Plains* (Boston: Houghton Mifflin, 1936), p. 493.

13. Isak Dinesen, *Out of Africa* (New York: Vintage Books, 1972), pp. 278–83.

14. Harold B. Barclay, *The Role of the Horse in Man's Culture* (London: J. A. Allen, 1980), pp. 369–70.

15. Frank Trippett, *The First Horsemen* (New York: Time-Life Books, 1974), p. 103.

16. J. M. Aynard, "Animals in Mesopotamia," in *Animals in Archaeology*, ed. A. Houghton Brodrick (London: Barrie & Jenkins, 1972), p. 65.

17. Elizabeth Atwood Lawrence, *Hoofbeats and Society: Studies of Human-Horse Interactions* (Bloomington: Indiana University Press, 1985), pp. 116–73.

18. Barclay, *Horse in Man's Culture*, p. 340.

19. Elizabeth Atwood Lawrence, *Rodeo: An Anthropologist Looks at the Wild and the Tame* (Chicago: University of Chicago Press, 1984), pp. 49–82.

20. John Cholis, "John Wayne, Cattleman," *Persimmon Hill* 7(1977):29.

21. E. C. Abbott (Teddy Blue) and Helena Huntington Smith, *We Pointed Them North: Recollections of a Cowpuncher* (New York: Farrar & Rinehart, 1939), p. 247.

22. James F. Downs, "Domestication: An Examination of the Changing Social Relationships Between Man and Animals," *Kroeber Anthropological Society Papers* 22(1960):30–31.

23. Emilio Willems, "Acculturation and the Horse Complex Among German-Brazilians," *American Anthropologist* 46(1944):160–61.

24. A. L. Kroeber, *Anthropology* (New York: Harcourt, Brace, 1948), p. 497.

25. Ibid., p. 502.

26. Lawrence, *Hoofbeats*, pp. 49, 146, 149, 151.

27. William G. Carr, *Man and Animal: Man Through His Art* (Greenwich, Conn.: New York Graphic Society, 1965), vol. 3, p. 48; J. C. Cooper, *An Illustrated Encyclopaedia of Traditional Symbols* (London: Thames and Hudson, 1978), p. 85; M. Oldfield Howey, *The Horse in Magic and Myth* (New York: Castle Books, 1958), pp. 114–25, LeRoy Neiman, *Horses* (New York: Abrams, 1979), p. 321; Beryl Rowland, *Animals With Human Faces: A Guide to Animal Symbolism* (Knoxville: University of Tennessee Press, 1973), p. 110.

28. Ronald Blythe, *Akenfield* (New York: Pantheon, 1969), p. 18.

29. J. Frank Dobie, *The Mustangs* (Boston: Little, Brown, 1952), p. xiii.

30. Edward Hall, *The Dance of Life* (Garden City, N.Y.: Doubleday, 1983), pp. 39–40.

31. Elias Canetti, *Crowds and Power* (New York: Continuum, 1978), p. 397.

32. Lawrence, *Hoofbeats*, pp. 148–49.

33. Barclay, *Horse in Man's Culture*, p. 358; Clutton-Brock, *Domesticated Animals From Early Times*, p. 86.

34. Lawrence, *Hoofbeats*, p. 158.

35. Zeuner, *History of Domesticated Animals*, p. 329.

36. Clutton-Brock, *Domesticated Animals From Early Times*, p. 86.

37. Plutarch, *The Age of Alexander* (New York: Penguin Books, 1980), pp. 257–58.

38. Stephen Vincent Benet, *John Brown's Body* (New York: Rinehart, 1955), pp. 170–71.

39. Elizabeth Atwood Lawrence, *His Very Silence Speaks: Comanche—The Horse Who Survived Custer's Last Stand* (Detroit: Wayne State University Press, 1989), pp. 308, 310–16, 319.

40. A. J. R. Lamb, *The Story of the Horse* (London: Alexander Maclehose & Co., 1938), pp. 193–94.

41. Elizabeth B. Custer, *Following the Guidon* (New York: Harper & Brothers, 1890), pp. 326–27.

42. Homer, *The Iliad* (New York: Penguin Books, 1986), pp. 327–28, 419–20.

43. Jilly Cooper, *Animals in War* (London: William Heinemann Ltd., 1983), p. 47.

44. Fanny Kemble Wister, ed., *Owen Wister Out West: His Journals and Letters* (Chicago: University of Chicago Press, 1958), pp. 108–9.

45. Peter Shaffer, *Equus* (New York: Atheneum, 1974).

46. Guy de Maupassant, "Coco," in *The Book of Horses*, ed. Fred Urquhart (New York: William Morrow and Co., 1981), pp. 15–19.

47. Leo Tolstoy, "Strider," in *The Portable Tolstoy*, ed. John Bayley (New York: Penguin Books, 1978), pp. 435–74.

48. The Chelsea Theater Center production of *Strider*, adapted by Mark Rozovsky from Tolstoy's story, played at the Helen Hayes Theatre in New York.

49. R. B. Cunninghame Graham, *The Horses of the Conquest* (Norman: University of Oklahoma Press, 1949), p. 11.

50. Gale Stubbs McClung, ed., "Horse Sense,"

Mount Holyoke Alumnae Quarterly LXX, no. 1 (1986):43.

51. Owen Wister, "The Evolution of the Cow Puncher," in *My Dear Wister: The Frederic Remington–Owen Wister Letters*, ed. Ben M. Vorpahl (Palo Alto: American West, 1972), p. 81.

52. Robert H. Lowie, *Indians of the Plains* (Garden City, N.Y.: Natural History Press, 1963), p. 44.

53. Lawrence, *Hoofbeats*, pp. 24–54.

54. E. Daumas, *The Horses of the Sahara* (Austin: University of Texas Press, 1968), pp. 7, 28, 29, 31, 32–33.

55. Jean-Paul Clebert, *The Gypsies* (London: Vista, 1963), p. xvii.

56. Seth-Smith, *Horse in Art and History*, p. 312; Clebert, *The Gypsies*, p. 102.

57. Vesey-Fitzgerald, *Book of the Horse*, p. 29.

58. Bart McDowell, *Gypsies: Wanderers of the World* (Washington, D.C.: National Geographic Society, 1970), p. 103; Clebert, *The Gypsies*, p. 103; Kamill Erdöes, "Gypsy Horse Dealers in Hungary," *Journal of the Gypsy Lore Society* 38, nos. 1–2(1959):3.

59. Jonathan Swift, *Gulliver's Travels* (New York: Penguin Books, 1985), p. 287.

60. Robert Hughes, "A Vision of Four-Legged Order," *Time* 124, no. 21(1984):132–33.

61. William Shakespeare, *Macbeth* (New York: Amsco, 1972), pp. 73–75.

62. Mircea Eliade, *Shamanism* (Princeton: Princeton University Press, 1974), pp. 173, 174, 467.

Lewis W. Hine. Untitled. May 1912. Silver print, 3½ × 4½"

THE HORSE IN PHOTOGRAPHS

BY GERALD LANG AND LEE MARKS

More than fifteen thousand years ago, prehistoric people made drawings of horses running across the walls of the Lascaux Caves in southern France. Although the motivating force of this endeavor was probably not art but rather magic ritual, to insure successful hunts of the horse as a means of sustenance, these drawings were the ancestors of a great collaboration between the human race and the horse that was to evolve into later expressions of art. Over the centuries, painting, drawing, sculpture, and printmaking richly explored this most versatile of animals and its relationship to human beings. In the mid-nineteenth century, yet another medium presented itself in photography, the miraculous invention that revolutionized forever the perception of reality.

There is a significant relationship between the development of photography and the changing role of the horse. When the invention of photography was announced in 1839, the horse was a part of everyday existence. Indispensable as a means of traction and transport, it was vital to hunting, farming, travel, war, and conquest. More than any other nonhuman species, the horse had directly influenced and altered the course of human history, and it was inconceivable in 1839 to envision a world without horses. However, in the years since, as photography has grown in influence, the role of the horse has shifted dramatically from a vehicle of labor to one of sport and leisure. In this collection of images, which traces the progress of photography from the most primitive calotypes and daguerreotypes of the earliest practitioners to today's computer-generated imagery, it is evident that the invention of photography represented but one aspect of the advancing technological movement that ultimately caused the horse to lose its central place in society.

As a participant in the everyday life of 1839, the horse naturally became a subject for the new medium of photography. To photograph any animal was extremely difficult at first. The earliest photographs required exposures sometimes as long as fifteen minutes to compensate for the primitive lenses and the slow speed of the light-sensitive materials available in the first decade of the medium. Images of subjects that could not remain still were virtually impossible, and pictures made outside the studio were rare. Louis-Auguste Bisson's *The Saddler* (plate 1), one of the earliest photographs of any animal, launched the tradition of nineteenth-century horse portraiture in photography. Typically, the horse was represented in strict profile and was held stationary by its master or groom. Alternatively, photographers portrayed dead subjects preserved by taxidermy, sleeping animals, or inanimate but evocative objects such as the rocking horse by William Henry Fox Talbot (plate 2). It was highly unusual to see "action" images like the anonymous American daguerreotype of a farrier shoeing a horse (plate 5).

Frederick Scott Archer's discovery of the wet collodion-on-glass process in 1851 liberated photography by reducing exposure times and improving detail in prints. While still lacking the ability to stop action, the process suggested the potential for representing spontaneity and movement. Mayer and Pierson's uncropped portrait of the Prince Imperial on his pony (plate 8) combines the traditional stationary attitude of an official portrait with a more casual and natural mood, suggested by the presence of the moving dog and the young boy's father, Napoleon III, standing at the right. A few years later, Julia Margaret Cameron's snapshot-like image of the Bowden-Smiths in Ceylon (plate 12) and C. Famin's impressionistic interpretation of the swish of a horse's tail (plate 13) would become possible with the use of collodion. The new process

also gave the photographer the ability to show the horse both at work and at war.

Where there were armies, there were horses. From its earliest days, the horse was a tool of power and conquest, participating in war as both partner and casualty. Nineteenth-century photographers recognized the animal's heroic contributions and recorded its image with the honor and respect accorded human heroes. Roger Fenton's *Lieutenant General Barnard's Horse* (plate 15), Gustave Le Gray's *The Camp at Châlons* (plate 16), and Confederate photographer Michael Miley's *General Robert E. Lee on Traveller* (plate 17) speak of the horse and war. While these pictures could not yet document the charge of the cavalry, they touch upon the relationship of man and horse within an environment of confrontation and conflict and, at times, as in Alexander Gardner's 1862 image of the dead horse on the battlefield at Antietam (plate 19), reveal the result.

Photography's ability to record objects and events in clear, factual terms made the medium an ideal scientific tool. As the technical process improved, the study of motion became possible. It was because of photography that, after thousands of years of interaction with the horse, people were at last shown exactly how a horse moved. Eadweard Muybridge's experimentation with the photography of movement in the 1870s provided the context for the most celebrated episode between the horse and photography (plate 33). Leland Stanford, former governor of California, president of the Central Pacific Railway, and owner of the Great Palo Alto Breeding Ranch, commissioned Muybridge to determine through photography whether his trotter Occident, when moving at full gallop, ever had all four feet off the ground. Using a battery of cameras arranged in rows and triggering the shutters electromagnetically, Muybridge proved that indeed all four feet left the ground at one time, but not in the assumed "rocking-horse" configuration to which painters and sculptors in history had always subscribed. (The photo finish that determines today's horse-racing winners is a direct descendant of this closeup analysis of motion.)

Inspired by Muybridge's studies, the Frenchman Etienne-Jules Marey invented in 1887 the chronophotographic camera, which could record the fluid motion of a trotting horse on a roll of light-sensitized film (plate 34); this machine was the ancestor of the motion-picture camera. In the 1930s, Dr. Harold Edgerton further increased photography's ability to record movement by developing a stroboscopic device whose brief and intense illuminations allowed the photographer to actually render visible such invisible occurrences as a drop of milk splashing or the moment of impact between foot and football. By synchronizing the flash of the strobe with the movement of the object, one could record either all phases of an object's movement or one quick moment such as the fall of a cowboy from a bucking bronco (plate 84).

In addition to Muybridge's work, which opened up possibilities for the camera's use as a scientific tool, another development in the late nineteenth century was to have long-lasting effects on the medium. The gelatin dry plate, introduced in 1871, was presensitized for the photographer's immediate use, and therefore a portable darkroom was no longer a necessity for on-the-spot developing of negatives made outside the studio. These new plates were also more sensitive to light, enabling photographers to use faster shutter speeds and capture such action sequences as Louis-Jean Delton's images from *Le Tour du Bois* (plate 35). The technical improvements provided by the dry plate led to the invention of the hand-held camera, which was to bring new freedom to the making of photographs. In 1888, George Eastman introduced the first roll-film Kodak camera. His famous slogan, "You push the button, we do the rest," signaled that photography was available to, and simple enough for, the public at large. *Horse Portrait: Colorado* (plate 58) was made with a Kodak #2 camera about 1890 by an unknown, probably amateur, photographer.

While the technological advances of the late nineteenth century were quickly putting cameras into the hands of amateurs, the role of the horse in society was changing more slowly. Contrary to what one might expect, the tasks of the working horse had not changed radically with the invention of the steam engine and the subsequent Industrial Revolution. Indeed, these developments actually increased the need for horses. By the turn of the century, the horse population in the United States was approaching its greatest numbers; by World War I,

there would be one horse for every three people. Such massive engineering feats as the building of the railroads would have been impossible without the horse to haul men, machinery, and materials. Frank Jay Haynes's *Iron Car Horse "Nig" at Last Spike* of 1883 (plate 30) attests to the horse's indispensability in this regard. Seventy-five years later, in his photograph *"Maud" Bows to the Virginia Creeper* (plate 120), O. Winston Link poignantly illustrates a horse appearing to bow in deference to the arrival of the "iron horse."

The invention of the internal combustion engine and the development of the automobile were the key advances that accelerated the transition of an essentially agrarian society to a technological one. The horse gradually lost its utilitarian function: the automobile replaced it in cities, and equipment became more and more mechanized on farms. For eight years beginning in 1882, the Englishman Peter Henry Emerson studied the tidal areas of East Anglia to document the preindustrial customs and traditions of a disappearing way of life. In *The Clay-Mill* and *A Stiff Pull* (plates 38, 39), the horses are large and powerful, lending an air of strength and commitment in support of a poor but noble existence. Shortly afterward, in images like *The Street—Design for a Poster* of 1903 (plate 50), Alfred Stieglitz commemorated the transition of the American city from the nineteenth century to the twentieth, from the picturesque to the modern. Frederick Brehm's 1910 panoramic portrait of police on horseback, on bicycles, and in automobiles also predicted the impending change (plate 57). The horses in Berenice Abbott's 1929 *The El at Columbus Avenue and Broadway* (plate 75) and in Robert Doisneau's 1969 *Les Embarras des Petits Champs* (plate 76) are silent. Gone are their sounds and smells, which had filled the city. Elevated above daily life, in which they no longer participate, they are transformed into objects of our imagination. In war, too, the cavalry ultimately gave way to armored tanks. Robert Capa's photograph of 1936 from the Spanish Civil War, *Soldiers of the International Brigade* (plate 68), illustrates one of the final appearances of cavalry on active rather than ceremonial duty.

For some cultures, the horse will always remain a metaphor of their origins and existence, whether or not they are forced ultimately to abandon the way of life it represents. As part of his thirty-year undertaking to document the Indians of North America, Edward Curtis photographed a young boy on the statuesque mount Medicine Hat Horse (plate 26). Although by 1926, when this photograph was made, the Indian nations had long been organized on reservations by the government, the image metaphorically depicts a proud and once-powerful heritage.

More recently, photographers have continued to document horse-owning cultures, often outside the mainstream, that could vanish or change substantially under the pressures of a society in constant flux. Gordon Parks's 1946 image of an Amish carriage and barn (plate 119) evokes one such group, devoted to maintaining its religious beliefs and simple way of life. In Alen MacWeeney's essay on the Irish tinkers outside of Dublin (plates 115, 117) and Josef Koudelka's study of the Romanian Gypsies (plate 114), traditions and myths of the horse are kept alive for succeeding generations. Koudelka's photograph of the man and horse linked in private dialogue reflects the abiding spiritual bond between the two; Mac-Weeney's image of the glowing white pony surrounded by admirers displays an intense pride of ownership as well as the central position the horse occupies in this unique society of people. Frozen by the light of an electronic flash, the bucking horse in Garry Winogrand's 1974 photograph (plate 123) preserves the contemporary tradition of the cowboy, while Laton Huffman's 1894 image *Andy Speelman, Ekalaka, Saddling a Wild Horse* (plate 29) and Elizabeth Roberts's 1900 picture *Frank Roberts With Horse Tied* (plate 27) document the "real" cowboy of the American West, whose era was on the wane by the beginning of the twentieth century.

The horse has served as a vehicle of sport for centuries, since shortly after its domestication by man. Greek literature discusses chariot racing as early as 600 B.C., the ancient Olympiads included competitions testing the dexterity of horse and rider, and the Persians played a form of polo in the fourth century B.C. Photography, from its earliest days, has been used to record sports, including those involving the horse. The daguerreotype of the polo pony is an early example (plate 6).

Later, the wet-collodion process made it easier for C. Reid to capture the essence of the fox hunt; photographing from afar, he was able to obscure the small movements of hounds and horse in the overall view (plate 36). Continued technical advances in cameras and film eventually gave every sports photographer the opportunity to capture the thrill of the action—to reveal the fraction of a second the eye cannot see. The Bowden Brothers' *Polo Tournament*, c. 1900 (plate 88), Hein Gorney's *The Jump*, c. 1930 (plate 62), and Aubrey Bodine's *Maryland Hunt Cup*, c. 1950 (plate 93), record such fleeting instants. The breathtaking drama, speed, and effort of Thoroughbred and harness racing are conveyed in Alexander Rodchenko's *Jockeys* of 1935 and Agnès Bonnot's 1984 image *Hippodrome de Vincennes* (plates 87, 92).

Many twentieth-century photographers have been especially sensitive to the artistic possibilities inherent in the image of the horse—in its physique, its accoutrements, and its mythology. Turning away from social documentation at the beginning of the century, the Photo-Secessionist followers of Alfred Stieglitz sought the acknowledgment of photography as a fine art and used the horse as a motif in their often soft-focus, painterly images, as in the work of Frank Eugene, George Seeley, and Harry C. Rubincam (plates 47, 48, 52). Later on, in the twenties, Manuel Alvarez Bravo used the motif in his photograph of carousel horses to surrealistically illuminate an aspect of Mexican folklore (plate 65). Modernist photographers of the twenties and thirties like Paul Outerbridge, Walker Evans, Berenice Abbott, and Ilse Bing applied the equine image to their vision of an ever-shifting, asymmetrical world. Although the horse had disappeared from the streets, evocative traces of it remain in the torn poster of Walker Evans (plate 78), the shop sign of Ilse Bing (plate 66), and the equestrian still life of Paul Outerbridge (plate 90). In Irving Penn's *Pulquería Decoration, Mexico* (plate 79), Edward Weston's *Salinas, Horses for Sale* (plate 80), and Wright Morris's *Bedroom, Home Place* (plate 82), fragments of horse imagery represent the art of the vernacular, the indigenous folk art decorating the humble structures of rural settings.

In the current arena of social documentation, some contemporary photographers have employed the horse in the service of politics, specifically to comment on the impact of human beings on the environment. The notion of the endangered species had been suggested earlier in the photographs of Thurman Rotan and Martine Franck (plates 73, 74), images clearly indicating the encroachment of city and industry on nature, but Richard Misrach jars our moral conscience about the ravages of environmental pollution in his series on dead-animal pits in the American desert (plate 143). Barbara Norfleet, another photographer associated with the new environmental photography, explores the often-confrontational relationship between human beings and the other animals who share the earth. In a recent series of photographs, Norfleet surprises horses, dogs, and smaller wild animals who venture curiously into a landscape furnished with human artifacts (plate 148).

Other contemporary photographers have appropriated the horse in a more artistically self-conscious way, to explore formal concerns in their work and expand the psychological limits of the photographic process. They have chosen to look inward, stimulated by the picture-making process of the mind. David Levinthal (plate 150) and Richard Prince (plate 152) have portrayed the horse as a symbol of popular culture, seizing on the myths the animal helps to perpetuate about vanished realities in movies, television, and advertising. Through a more painterly approach, Doug and Mike Starn (plate 147), Holly Roberts (plate 149), and Betty Hahn (plate 151) have reworked the image of the horse into comprehensive series, emphasizing form over content and combining photography with other media such as painting and collage.

The year 1992 will mark the five-hundredth anniversary of Columbus's reintroduction of the horse to America. Encompassing more than the utilitarian functions of work, transport, and sport, the horse is part of our spiritual imagination as well and symbolizes beauty, energy, the force of nature, and the spirit of freedom. For centuries, this animal has held the most esteemed position of any in our society. And the history of photography richly reflects our fascination with the horse. Motivated by cultural, documentary, scientific, and aesthetic concerns, masters and anonymous photographers alike have explored the equine world. Whether seen as document, symbol, or metaphor, the image of the horse in these photographs provides an illuminating commentary on our lives, our spirit, and our dreams.

The Saddler,

1. Louis-Auguste Bisson.
The Saddler. c. 1841.
Half-plate daguerreotype, handcolored

2. WILLIAM HENRY FOX TALBOT.
ROCKING HORSE AT LACOCK ABBEY. 1843.
SALT PRINT FROM PAPER
NEGATIVE, 5¼ × 7½"

3. CHARLES CLIFFORD.
SIXTEENTH-CENTURY CHINESE SADDLE.
EARLY 1860s.
ALBUMEN PRINT FROM
WET COLLODION-ON-GLASS
NEGATIVE, 12¾ × 10⅜"

4. NEVIL STORY-MASKELYNE.
SULTAN. MID-1850s.
SALT PRINT FROM
WET COLLODION-ON-GLASS
NEGATIVE, 5¾ × 6¾"

5. Photographer unknown.
The Farrier. 1848–50.
Sixth-plate daguerreotype

6. J. Newman.
Polo Pony. c. 1850.
Half-plate daguerreotype

7. JEAN-GABRIEL EYNARD-LULLIN AND JEAN RION.
M. EYNARD, GRISELDA, FÉLIX. C. 1843—52.
FULL-PLATE DAGUERREOTYPE

8. MAYER & PIERSON
(HÉRIBERT MAYER AND LOUIS PIERSON).
THE PRINCE IMPERIAL ON HIS PONY
BEING PHOTOGRAPHED. C. 1859.
ALBUMEN PRINT FROM
WET COLLODION-ON-GLASS
NEGATIVE, 6⅝ × 6⅝"

9. Photographer unknown.
Untitled. 1870s.
Albumen print from
wet collodion-on-glass
negative, 8⅛ × 6″

10. Adrien Tournachon.
Mouton. c. 1855.
Albumen print from paper
negative, 6⅞ × 8⅞"

11. George Francis Schreiber.
Untitled. c. 1881.
Platinum print,
handcolored, 19⅝ × 27½″

12. JULIA MARGARET CAMERON (ATTRIBUTED).
THE BOWDEN-SMITHS AT DARLEY
HOUSE, COLOMBO, CEYLON. 1873.
ALBUMEN PRINT FROM WET
COLLODION-ON-GLASS
NEGATIVE, 5⅜ × 7⅞″

13. C. FAMIN.
HORSE. C. 1874.
ALBUMEN PRINT FROM
WET COLLODION-ON-GLASS
NEGATIVE, 6⅜ × 4¾″

14. NADAR (GASPARD-FÉLIX TOURNACHON).
UNTITLED. C. 1865.
ALBUMEN PRINT FROM
WET COLLODION-ON-GLASS
NEGATIVE, 8 × 9¾"

15. ROGER FENTON.
LIEUTENANT GENERAL BARNARD'S HORSE,
GRANDSON OF MARENGO. 1855.
SALT PRINT FROM WET
COLLODION-ON-GLASS
NEGATIVE, 6 × 5⅞"

16. GUSTAVE LE GRAY.
THE CAMP AT CHÂLONS, MANEUVERS
OF OCTOBER 3, 1857.
ALBUMEN PRINT FROM WET
COLLODION-ON-GLASS
NEGATIVE, 11⅛ × 14⅜″

17. MICHAEL MILEY.
GENERAL ROBERT E. LEE ON TRAVELLER. 1868.
ALBUMEN PRINT FROM
WET COLLODION-ON-GLASS
NEGATIVE, 6⅜ × 8⅞"

18. Andrew J. Russell.
Rebel Caisson Destroyed by
Federal Shells, at
Fredericksburg, May 3, 1863.
Albumen print from
wet collodion-on-glass
negative, 9 × 12¾"

19. Alexander Gardner.
Dead Horse of a Confederate Colonel,
Near the East Woods, on or About
September 20, 1862.
Stereo view, albumen print from
wet collodion-on-glass negative

20. TIMOTHY O'SULLIVAN.
THE HALT. 1864.
ALBUMEN PRINT FROM
WET COLLODION-ON-GLASS
NEGATIVE, 6¾ × 8⅞"

21. DAVID KNOX.
FORGE SCENE, FRONT OF
PETERSBURG, AUGUST, 1864.
ALBUMEN PRINT FROM
WET COLLODION-ON-GLASS
NEGATIVE, 6⅞ × 8⅞"

22. MATHEW B. BRADY.
GENERAL RAWLINS'S HORSE; TAKEN AT
COLD HARBOR, VIRGINIA, JUNE 14, 1864.
STEREO VIEW, ALBUMEN PRINT FROM
WET COLLODION-ON-GLASS NEGATIVE

23. PHOTOGRAPHER UNKNOWN.
THE HORSE DRAWING. 1870S.
TWO SIXTH-PLATE TINTYPES

24. FRANK B. FISKE.
TIPIS, STANDING ROCK
INDIAN RESERVATION. N.D.
SILVER PRINT, 4½ × 6⅜"

25. D. F. BARRY.
COMANCHE. 1870S.
CABINET CARD, ALBUMEN
PRINT FROM WET
COLLODION-ON-GLASS NEGATIVE, 4 × 6"

26. Edward S. Curtis.
A Painted Tipi—Assiniboin. 1926.
Photogravure, 11⅜ × 15¾"

27. ELIZABETH ROBERTS.
FRANK ROBERTS WITH HORSE TIED,
SLOPE COUNTY, N.D. C. 1910.
SILVER PRINT, 7⅜ × 7⅜"

28. PHOTOGRAPHER UNKNOWN.
JESSE JAMES ON HORSEBACK. C. 1870.
TINTYPE, 2⅝ × 3¾"

29. Laton A. Huffman.
Andy Speelman, Ekalaka,
Saddling a Wild Horse. 1894.
Collotype, 10 × 8"

45

1542.—IRON CAR HORSE "NIG," AND TRACKLAYERS

30. FRANK JAY HAYNES.
IRON CAR HORSE "NIG" AT
LAST SPIKE, VILLARD
EXCURSION, SEPT. 8, 1883.
ALBUMEN PRINT FROM
WET COLLODION-ON-GLASS
NEGATIVE, 6⅝ × 9⅞"

31. GIUSEPPE PRIMOLI.
ANNIE OAKLEY, ROME, MARCH 1890.
SILVER PRINT, 7 × 4¾"

32. PHOTOGRAPHER UNKNOWN.
BUFFALO BILL. C. 1887.
STEREO VIEW, ALBUMEN PRINT FROM
WET COLLODION-ON-GLASS NEGATIVE

731. WILD WEST.

33. Eadweard Muybridge.
Plate 640 from Animal Locomotion. 1887.
Collotype, 9⅞×12″

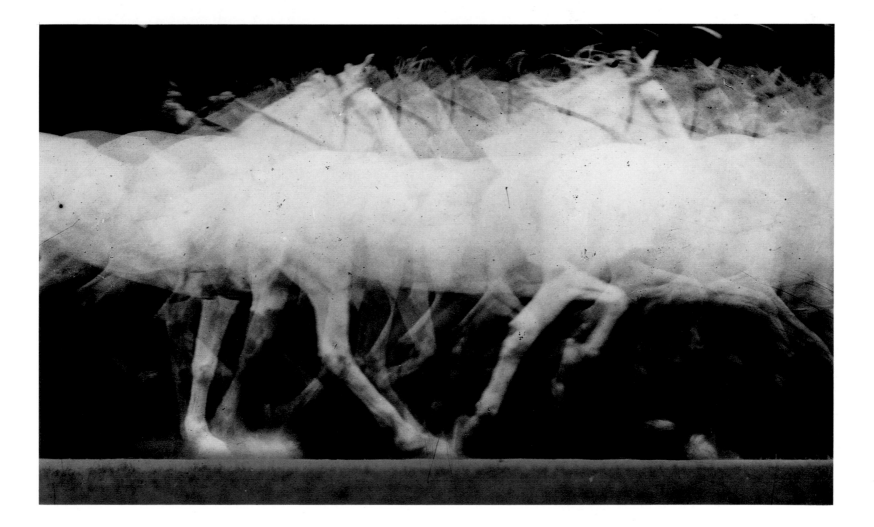

34. ETIENNE-JULES MAREY.
CHEVAL AU TROT. 1886.
ALBUMEN PRINT, 5½ × 9⅛"

35. Louis-Jean Delton.
Woman on Horseback,
Taking a Jump. 1884.
Albumen prints from
glass-plate negatives,
each 4⅛ × 3¾"

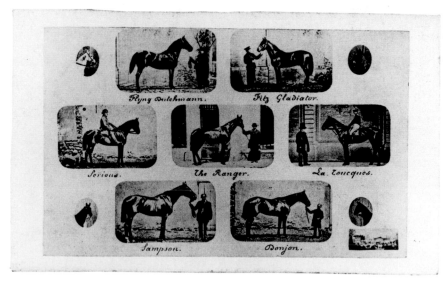

36. C. REID.
UNTITLED. 1880S.
ALBUMEN PRINT FROM
WET COLLODION-ON-GLASS
NEGATIVE, 4½ × 7⅛"

37. PHOTOGRAPHER UNKNOWN.
UNTITLED. 1860S.
CARTE-DE-VISITE,
ALBUMEN PRINTS FROM WET
COLLODION-ON-GLASS NEGATIVES

38. PETER HENRY EMERSON.
THE CLAY-MILL (NORFOLK). BEFORE 1888.
PHOTOGRAVURE, 7⅞ × 11⅜"

39. Peter Henry Emerson.
A Stiff Pull. Before 1888.
Photogravure, 8⅛ × 11¼"

40. Frank M. Sutcliffe.
Untitled. 1870s.
Albumen print from
wet collodion-on-glass
negative, 5¼ × 7¾"

41. CARLO PONTI.
HORSES OF SAINT MARK'S, VENICE. C. 1860.
ALBUMEN PRINT FROM
WET COLLODION-ON-GLASS
NEGATIVE, 10¾ × 13½"

42. WALTER HEGE.
REARING HORSE—WEST FRIEZE, PARTHENON. C. 1928.
SILVER PRINT, 11⅜ × 8¾"

43. W. A. MANSELL & CO.
PANEL FROM PARTHENON FRIEZE. 1860S.
ALBUMEN PRINT FROM
WET COLLODION-ON-GLASS
NEGATIVE, 9¼ × 8⅛"

44. CHARLES NÈGRE.
FAME RIDING PEGASUS, TUILERIES GARDENS, PARIS. 1859.
ALBUMEN PRINT FROM WET COLLODION-ON-GLASS
NEGATIVE, 17½ × 14″

45. EUGÈNE ATGET.
LUXEMBOURG,
FONTAINE CARPEAUX.
1901—2. ALBUMEN PRINT
FROM GLASS-PLATE
NEGATIVE, 9⅜ × 7″

56

46. ALVIN LANGDON COBURN.
TREVI FOUNTAIN, ROME. 1906.
GUM BICHROMATE/PLATINUM
PRINT, 11½ × 14⅜″

47. FRANK EUGENE.
HORSE. 1895.
PHOTOGRAVURE, 4⅛ × 8⅛″

48. GEORGE SEELEY.
YOUTH WITH HORSE. C. 1907.
PLATINUM PRINT, 9½ × 7⅝″

49. J. CRAIG ANNAN.
STIRLING CASTLE. 1906.
PHOTOGRAVURE, 5⅞ × 8½"

50. ALFRED STIEGLITZ.
THE STREET—DESIGN FOR A POSTER. 1903.
PHOTOGRAVURE, 18¾ × 12¾"

51. ALFRED STIEGLITZ.
GOING TO THE POST. 1904.
PHOTOGRAVURE, 12⅛ × 10⅜"

52. HARRY C. RUBINCAM.
IN THE CIRCUS. 1905.
PHOTOGRAVURE, 6⅛ × 7⅝"

53. PHOTOGRAPHER UNKNOWN.
EUNICE WINKLESS'S DIVE INTO POOL
OF WATER, PUEBLO, COLORADO, JULY 4, 1905.
SILVER PRINT, 7⅜ × 9½"

54. PHOTOGRAPHER UNKNOWN.
MAY WIRTH. C. 1915.
SILVER PRINT, 3⅝ × 3⅛"

55. PHOTOGRAPHER UNKNOWN.
UNTITLED. 1870S.
ALBUMEN PRINT FROM
WET COLLODION-ON-GLASS
NEGATIVE, 4⅛ × 5⅝"

56. FRANCES BENJAMIN JOHNSTON.
AGRICULTURE. ANIMAL LIFE.
STUDYING THE HORSE. 1899–1900.
PLATINUM PRINT, 7½ × 9½"

57. FREDERICK W. BREHM.
POLICE GROUP PORTRAIT. C. 1910.
SILVER PRINT, 9¼ × 22¼"

58. PHOTOGRAPHER UNKNOWN.
HORSE PORTRAIT: COLORADO. C. 1890.
SILVER PRINT, 3½″ DIAMETER

59. HILL AND WATKINS.
UNTITLED. 1890S.
IMPERIAL CABINET CARD,
ALBUMEN PRINT FROM WET
COLLODION-ON-GLASS
NEGATIVE, 7½ × 9¼″

60. Alfred Stieglitz.
Spiritual America. 1923.
Silver print, 4½ × 3½"

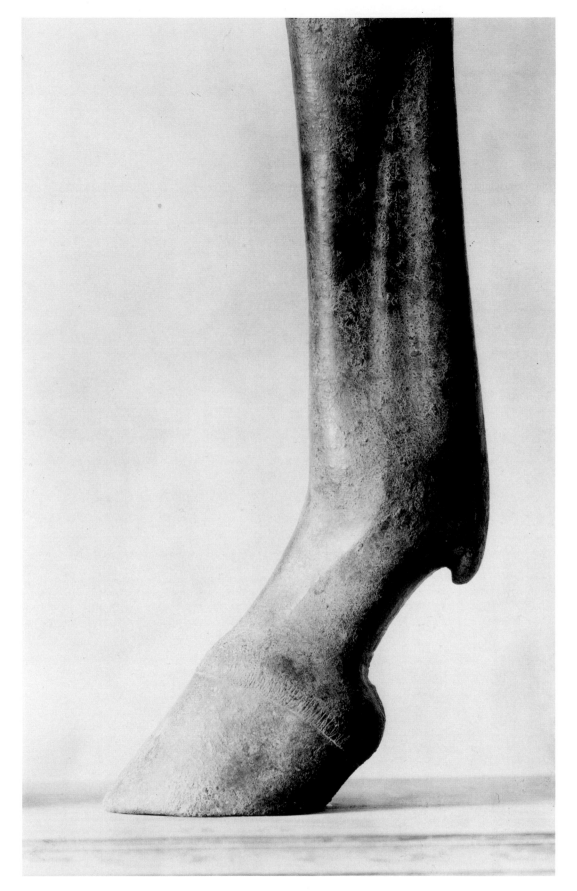

61. CLARENCE KENNEDY.
LEGEND HOOF OF A BRONZE HORSE
FOUND AT THE SAME TIME AS
THE CHARIOTEER AT DELPHI. 1928.
TONED SILVER PRINT, 10¼ × 6½"

62. HEIN GORNY.
THE JUMP. C. 1930.
SILVER PRINT, 9 × 6½"

63. Albert Renger-Patzsch.
Pferd am Priel. c. 1926.
Silver print, 9 × 6⅜″

64. Henri Cartier-Bresson.
Martigues, France. 1932—33.
Silver print, 8⅞ × 5⅞"

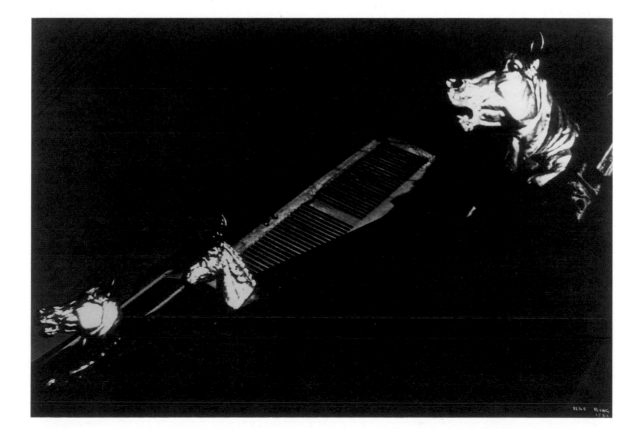

65. Manuel Alvarez Bravo.
Los Obstáculos. 1929.
Platinum print, 7 × 9¼"

66. Ilse Bing.
Shop Sign, Paris. 1933.
Silver print, 7¾ × 11⅛"

67. GOTTHARD SCHUH.
CAVALRY. C. 1938.
SILVER PRINT, 3½ × 11½"

68. ROBERT CAPA.
SOLDIERS OF THE INTERNATIONAL
BRIGADE, SPAIN. 1936.
SILVER PRINT, 7⅜ × 9⅜"

69. André Kertész.
Paris. 1927.
Six silver prints,
each 4½ × 6⅛"

70. Cas Oorthuys.
Untitled (Taxidermist's Horse). c. 1944.
Silver print, 7⅞ × 6⅝″

71. Paul Strand.
White Horse, Ranchos de Taos,
New Mexico. 1932.
Silver print, 9⅛ × 11½"

72. Martin Munkácsi.
Cody, Wyoming, Teton Range. 1938.
Silver print, 10⅜ × 13½"

73. Thurman Rotan.
San Antonio. 1932.
Silver print, 5¾ × 4⅜"

74. MARTINE FRANCK.
NEWCASTLE ON TYNE, ENGLAND. 1978.
SILVER PRINT, 5¾ × 8½"

79

75. BERENICE ABBOTT.
THE EL AT COLUMBUS AVENUE
AND BROADWAY. 1929.
SILVER PRINT, 6⅜ × 8¾"

76. Robert Doisneau.
Les Embarras des Petits Champs. 1969.
Silver print, 7¼ × 9¼"

77. Esther Bubley.
Rockefeller Center, N.Y. 1940s.
Silver print, 8⅝ × 13"

78. WALKER EVANS.
SOUTHEASTERN U.S. 1936.
SILVER PRINT, 8½ × 6½″

79. IRVING PENN.
PULQUERÍA DECORATION, MEXICO. 1942.
SILVER PRINT, 11 × 10¼″

80. EDWARD WESTON.
SALINAS, HORSES FOR SALE. 1939.
SILVER PRINT, 7½ × 9½"

81. WALKER EVANS.
STABLES, NATCHEZ, MISSISSIPPI. MARCH 1935.
SILVER PRINT, 10×8"

82. WRIGHT MORRIS.
BEDROOM, HOME PLACE. 1947.
SILVER PRINT, 8×10"

83. EDWARD WESTON.
K. B. DUDE RANCH. 1938.
SILVER PRINT, 7½ × 9½"

84. HAROLD E. EDGERTON.
RODEO. 1940.
SILVER PRINT, 8⅜ × 7"

85. Photographer unknown.
Triple Dead Heat, Windsor, 1923.
Silver print, 17 × 23⅜″

86. Edward Steichen.
Gallant Fox and Landry. 1930.
Silver print, 7⅝ × 9⅝"

87. ALEXANDER MIKHAILOVICH RODCHENKO.
JOCKEYS. 1935.
SILVER PRINT, 4 × 6″

88. BOWDEN BROTHERS, LONDON.
POLO TOURNAMENT, LONDON: WHITE'S
CLUB VS. BATH CLUB. C. 1900.
COLLODIO-CHLORIDE PRINT, 4¼ × 5⅞″

89. MAN RAY.
POLO PLAYER. C. 1935.
SILVER PRINT, 6⅜ × 8¾"

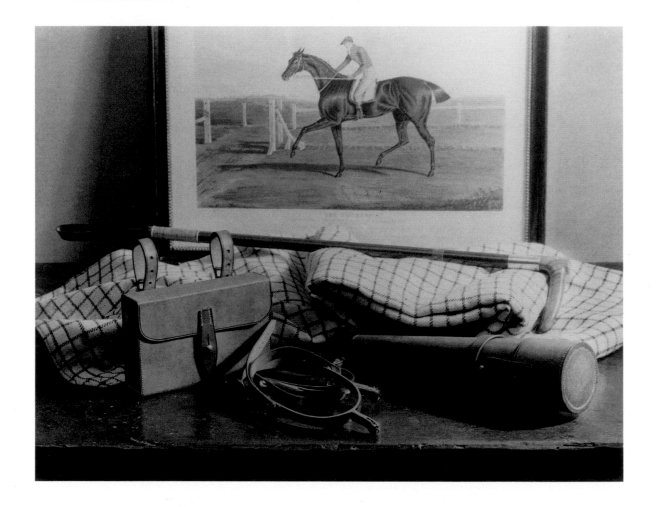

90. Paul Outerbridge, Jr.
Equestrian Still Life. 1924.
Platinum print, 4⅝ × 6″

91. BERENICE ABBOTT.
HARNESS SHOP HORSE. 1930.
SILVER PRINT, 9½ × 7½"

92. AGNÈS BONNOT.
HIPPODROME DE VINCENNES. 1984.
SILVER PRINT, 7 × 6⅝″

93. A. AUBREY BODINE.
MARYLAND HUNT CUP. C. 1950.
TONED SILVER PRINT, 13½ × 11″

94. MARION POST WOLCOTT.
SULKY RACE, MERCER COUNTY,
KENTUCKY. 1940.
SILVER PRINT, 7 × 9⅜″

95. Brassaï (Gyula Halász).
The Royal Show, England. 1959.
Silver print, 11⅜ × 9¼"

96. LEONARD FREED.
SALE OF THE YEARLINGS
IN DEAUVILLE, FRANCE. 1964.
SILVER PRINT, 10¼ × 14⅞″

97. Edward J. Steichen.
White. 1935.
Silver print, 7½ × 9½"

98. Ansel Adams.
Saddle. 1929.
Silver print, 6 × 8"

99. PAUL STRAND.
HARNESS, LUZZARA, ITALY. 1953.
SILVER PRINT, 9⅝ × 7⅝"

100. Bill Brandt.
The White Horse Near Westbury. c. 1946.
Silver print, 8¾ × 7½"

101. Walter Rosenblum.
Horse, Gaspé, Canada. 1949.
Silver print, 10½ × 13½"

102. Paul Strand.
Tir a'Mhurain, South
Uist, Hebrides. 1954.
Silver print, 9⅜ × 11⅜"

103. Robert Frank.
Valencia, Spain. 1951—52.
Silver print, 9¼ × 13¾"

104. Dorothea Lange.
Terrified Horse, Berryessa
Valley, California. 1956.
Silver print, 6⅝ × 9⅝″

105. ELLIOTT ERWITT.
BRAZIL. 1970.
SILVER PRINT, 8 × 12"

106. DENNIS STOCK.
THE ALAMO. 1959.
SILVER PRINT, 13¼ × 10½"

107. Henri Cartier-Bresson.
Stud Farm, Touques (Calvados). 1968.
Silver print, 6⅝ × 9⅞"

108. Eve Arnold.
The Misfits. 1960.
Silver print, 9⅞ × 6⅝″

109. David Hurn.
The Last of the Mustang
Round-ups, Arizona. 1980.
Silver print, 6¼ × 9⅜"

110. René Burri.
Gaucho, Argentina. 1958.
Silver print, 11⅝ × 7⅝″

111. Lucien Clergue.
La Pique, Nîmes. 1964.
Silver print, 11¾ × 8¼″

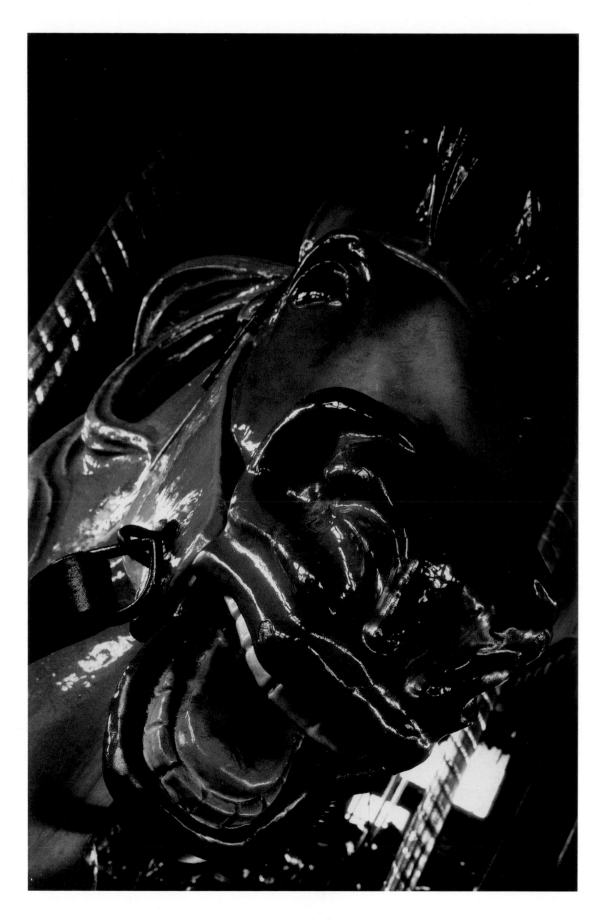

112. Peter Laytin.
Carousel Horse No. 1. 1972.
Silver print, 8¾ × 5⅝″

113. JOSEF KOUDELKA.
SPAIN. 1973.
SILVER PRINT, 5⅞ × 8⅞"

114. Josef Koudelka.
Romania. 1968.
Silver print, 6¼ × 9½"

115. Alen MacWeeney.
White Horse, Donegal. 1965.
Silver print, 8¼ × 8¼"

116. Bruce Davidson.
Welsh Pony. 1965.
Silver print, 6½ × 9⅞"

117. Alen MacWeeney.
White Pony, Clifden Horse
Fair, Ireland. 1965.
Silver print, 8½ × 8½"

118. ELIOT PORTER.
PAINTED HORSES ON BARN DOOR,
CUNDIYO, NEW MEXICO. 1961.
SILVER PRINT, 9½ × 7¼"

119. GORDON PARKS.
LANCASTER COUNTY BARNYARD OF
CHRISTIAN CLECK (?), AMISH VEGETABLE AND
TOBACCO FARMER NEAR COATESVILLE. APRIL 1946.
SILVER PRINT, 12½ × 9⅞"

120. O. WINSTON LINK.
"MAUD" BOWS TO THE VIRGINIA
CREEPER, GREEN COVE, VIRGINIA. 1956.
SILVER PRINT, 16 × 20"

121. JEROME LIEBLING.
BROWNING, MONTANA. 1962.
SILVER PRINT, 10⅛ × 10¼″

122. DANNY LYON.
THE BOSS, TEXAS. 1968.
SILVER PRINT, 5¾ × 8½″

123. GARRY WINOGRAND.
FORT WORTH, TEXAS. 1974.
SILVER PRINT, 6 × 9″

124. GEOFFREY WINNINGHAM.
SANDY WILSON, MISS NATIONAL APPALOOSA QUEEN, WITH "JOKERS WILD"
AND HIS TRAINER, HOUSTON LIVESTOCK SHOW. 1972.
SILVER PRINT, 7½ × 11¼″

125. AARON SISKIND.
OLD HORSE, CHILMARK 46. 1971.
SILVER PRINT, 9¾ × 9⅝″

126. Ralph Gibson.
Horse's Head and Hand. 1974.
Silver print, 12¾ × 8¼"

127. W. Eugene Smith.
Skull in Shadow. 1947.
Silver print, 12½ × 10½"

128. Lee Friedlander.
General Andrew Jackson, Lafayette
Park, Washington, D.C. 1973.
Silver print, 11 × 14"

129. RICHARD BENSON.
AUGUSTUS SAINT-GAUDENS'S MEMORIAL
TO THE MASSACHUSETTS 54TH REGIMENT. 1973.
PLATINUM PRINT, 11 × 14"

130. LINDA CONNOR.
SPANISH RIDER, CANYON
DE CHELLY, ARIZONA. 1987.
SILVER CONTACT PRINT
ON PRINTING-OUT PAPER,
GOLD-TONED, 8 × 10"

131. ELAINE MAYES.
NEW YORK THRUWAY,
CHRISTMAS (PEGASUS). 1972.
SILVER PRINT, 9⅝ × 6½"

132. HELEN LEVITT.
UNTITLED—CHALK DRAWINGS.
C. 1942.
SILVER PRINT, 8 × 5½"

133. OLIVIA PARKER.
CAROUSEL 1. 1982.
GELATIN-SILVER CONTACT PRINT
WITH SELENIUM TONING, 12 × 20″

134. SALLY MANN.
WINTER SQUASH. 1988.
SILVER PRINT, 6⅜ × 8¾"

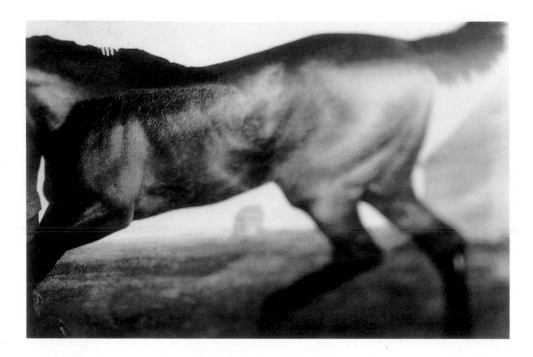

135. Eileen Toumanoff.
The Horse No. 1. 1987.
Silver print, 3⅜ × 5″

136. Ruth Thorne-Thomsen.
Horses, Illinois. 1976.
Toned silver contact print
from paper negative, 3¾ × 4¾″

137. JED DEVINE.
TOY HORSES ON CARPET. 1978.
PALLADIUM PRINT, 7½ × 9½"

138. WILLIE ANNE WRIGHT.
CIVIL WAR REDUX: FEDERAL
CAVALRY, GETTYSBURG. 1988.
SILVER PRINT, 3¾ × 4½"

139. Michael Spano.
City Cowboys, New York City. 1988.
Silver print from
eight-frame negative, 50 × 40"

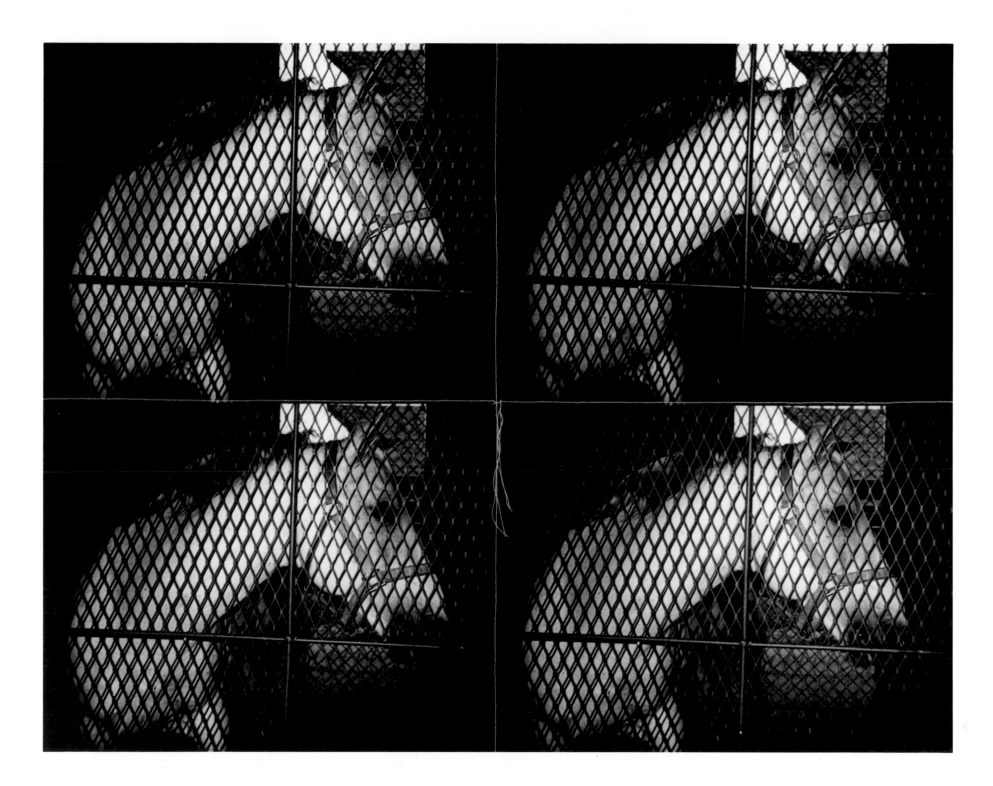

140. Andy Warhol.
Horse Behind Gate. 1976/1986.
Four silver prints sewn together, 22 × 28″

141. SYLVIA PLACHY.
NIGHT MARE. 1980.
SILVER PRINT, 5 × 7⅜″

142. ALEKSANDRAS MACIJAUSKAS.
IN THE VETERINARY CLINIC. 1978.
SILVER PRINT, 6⅜ × 9½″

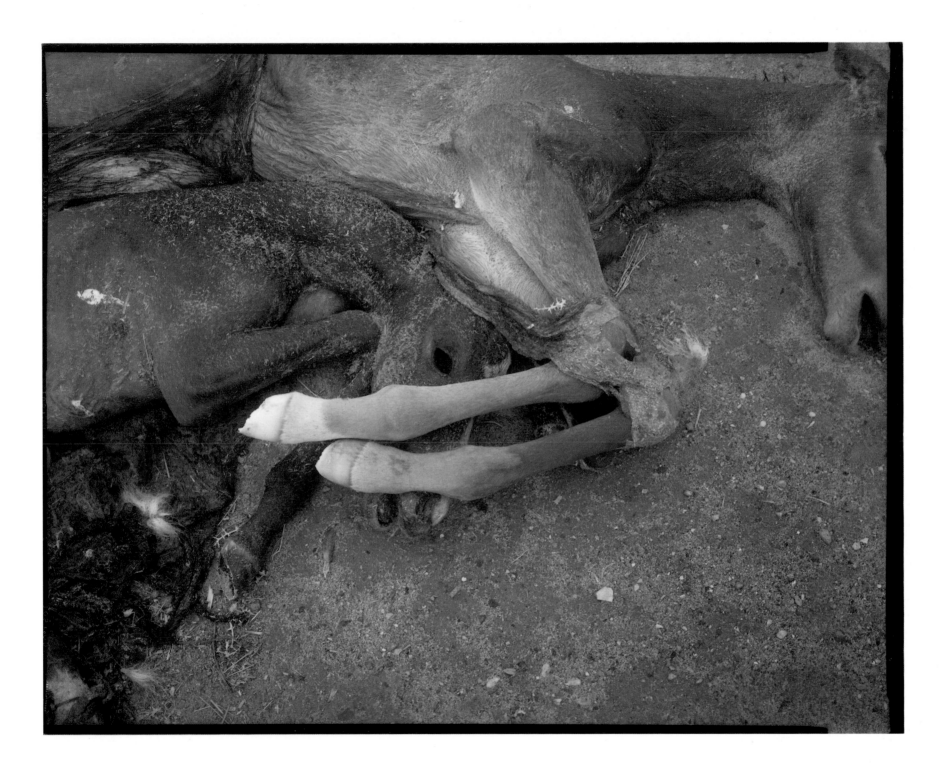

143. RICHARD MISRACH.
DEAD ANIMALS NO. 79. 1987.
EKTACOLOR PLUS PRINT, 40 × 50"

144. Richard H. Ross.
Deyrolle Taxidermy, Paris, France. 1985.
Ektacolor Plus print, 30 × 30″

145. Jan Groover.
Untitled (Angel and Horse Atop Column). 1987.
Type C print, 16¾ × 18½"

146. JOEL MEYEROWITZ.
SPAIN. 1967.
DYE TRANSFER PRINT, 15½ × 23½"

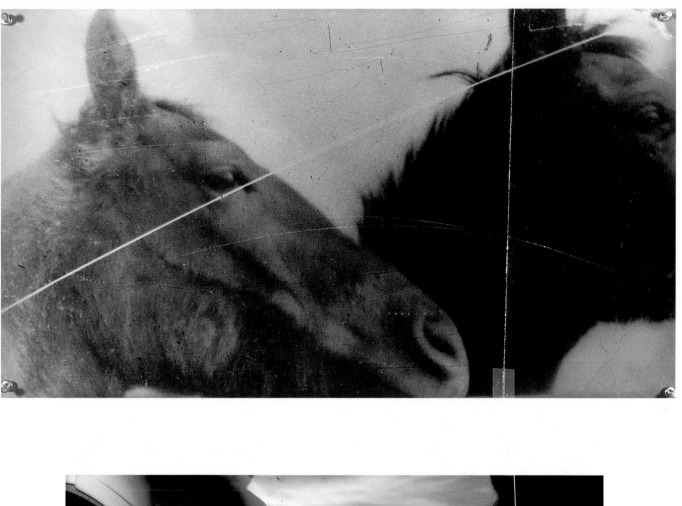

147. DOUG AND MIKE STARN.
HORSES. 1985—86.
TONED SILVER PRINT, TAPE, 14×24″

148. BARBARA NORFLEET.
TISBURY GREAT POND. 1985.
CIBACHROME PRINT, 16×20″

149. HOLLY ROBERTS.
FRISIAN STALLION. 1981.
OIL ON SILVER PRINT, 11 × 14″

150. DAVID LEVINTHAL.
UNTITLED (COWBOYS AND WESTERN LANDSCAPES). 1989.
COLOR INK-JET PROCESS
ON CANVAS, 72 × 72″

151. BETTY HAHN.
A STARRY NIGHT. 1975.
CYANOTYPE WITH WATERCOLOR AND
APPLIED SILVER STARS, 22 × 18″

152. RICHARD PRINCE.
UNTITLED—COWBOYS. 1986.
EKTACOLOR PRINT, 27 × 40"

NOTES ON THE PHOTOGRAPHS

By Lee Marks

Frontispiece: Hiro (Yasuhiro Wakabayashi). Japanese, b. 1930. *Running Horse, Montauk*, N.Y., *1955*. Silver print, 4¾ × 6½″. Courtesy Hiro

Born in Shanghai of Japanese parents, Hiro spent most of his early years in China, before moving to the United States at the age of twenty-three to begin a career in photography. Eventually he was hired by Richard Avedon who, realizing his assistant's brilliant potential, introduced Hiro to Alexey Brodovitch and *Harper's Bazaar.* During the sixties and seventies, Hiro was a dynamic participant in the innovative world of fashion and editorial magazine photography, championed by the art directors at *Harper's Bazaar.* He left the magazine in 1975 and became more and more absorbed in advertising photography as well as his own personal work, of which *Running Horse* is an early example. Departing from Hiro's typically controlled orchestration of subject matter and technique, this simple, previously unpublished image of a horse has no artifice, no technological wizardry; it is purely an unbridled horse running free.

Page 6: August Sander. German, 1876–1964. *Child on Horseback.* c. 1935. Silver print, 4⅝ × 6⅛″. Courtesy Sander Gallery, New York

In 1910, Sander opened a commercial portrait studio in Cologne and began the project, Man of the Twentieth Century, that would occupy him during the years of the Weimar Republic. He resolved to make a photographic compendium of the German people, ordered by profession, trade, and rank in society. Sixty of the portraits were published in 1929 in *Antlitz der Zeit* (Face of Our Time). In 1934, however, the government of the Third Reich had the book plates destroyed, and Sander was forced to abandon his individualistic portraits, which challenged the idealized images the Nazis revered. It was probably during his subsequent period of landscape and genre photography that Sander made this tender image of the tiny child on horseback.

Page 18: Lewis W. Hine. American, 1874–1940. Untitled. May 1912. Silver print, 3½ × 4½″. Gilman Paper Company Collection

From 1906 until 1917, Hine worked for the National Child Labor Committee, traveling over fifty thousand miles through much of the United States to photograph the exploitation of young children in the American labor force. Known for his editorializing captions, he wrote ironically of this atypical example of his work: "A Carolina colt living in Spartenberg Mill Settlement but unfortunately not put to work too early as the human colts are."

1. Louis-Auguste Bisson. French, 1814–1876. *The Saddler.* c. 1841. Half-plate daguerreotype, handcolored. Courtesy Hans P. Kraus, Jr., New York

Although best known for their large-format albumen prints made from wet collodion-on-glass negatives, Louis-Auguste Bisson and his brother, Auguste-Rosalie, began in the business of photography by opening a daguerreotype studio in Paris about 1840–41. Known as Bisson Frères, their studio specialized in portraiture. This daguerreotype of the horse called The Saddler is undoubtedly one of the earliest examples of Bisson's work and one of the earliest existing photographs of an animal. In the nineteenth century, long exposures were required to accommodate the slow speed of light-sensitive photographic materials. Therefore, images of live animals, especially made outside, were usually not possible unless the animals were photographed while sleeping or unless verisimilitude was suggested by the art of taxidermy.

2. William Henry Fox Talbot. English, 1800–1877. *Rocking Horse at Lacock Abbey.* 1843. Salt print from paper negative, 5¼ × 7½″. National Museum of Photography, Film and Television, Bradford, England

Simultaneous with the invention of the daguerreotype in Paris, Talbot announced in 1839 his early work with a technique that would ultimately develop into the calotype negative-positive process. Talbot's process had an advantage over the daguerreotype in that it produced a negative matrix for creating multiple copies of a single image, a feature that had important ramifications for the publication of photographs. A pioneer in publishing, Talbot produced, between June 1844 and April 1846, what is traditionally considered the first major book incorporating photographic plates with printed text, *The Pencil of Nature.* One of his claims for photography was its ability to record the form and texture of artworks, especially objects altered over time by erosion. Many of his early photographs depicted sculptural busts, glass, lace, and evocative objects such as the rocking horse. Symbols of childhood, the rocking horse and hobby horse have also been associated with transition and renewal in the various stages of life.

3. Charles Clifford. English, c. 1819–1863. *Sixteenth-century Chinese Saddle.* Early 1860s. Albumen print from wet collodion-on-glass negative, 12¾ × 10⅜″. Courtesy Mayer & Mayer, Galerie für Photographie, Stuttgart/Cologne

The widespread use of the saddle, with its framework of bone or metal and padding, is thought to have developed in Asia during the Han Dynasty, beginning about 200 B.C. These first saddles lacked stirrups, which would be added later by the Hindu descendants of the earliest effective tamers of horses, the Brahmins. This photograph of a Chinese saddle is the work of Charles Clifford, a professional photographer who worked in Madrid from 1852 until his death in 1863. In 1858, while still registered as official photographer to Queen Victoria, he also became the court photographer of Queen Isabella II of Spain. While his intent was probably documentary, Clifford's stark image of the Chinese saddle resonates with equestrian elegance.

4. Nevil Story-Maskelyne. English, 1823–1911. *Sultan.* Mid-1850s. Salt print from wet collodion-on-glass negative, 5¼ × 6¾″. Gilman Paper Company Collection

Despite his father's wishes that he make a career in law, Maskelyne also studied the sciences at Oxford and earnestly experimented with the chemistry of photography. He married a relative of William Henry Fox Talbot and became part of the serious and productive group of amateur photographers surrounding the inventor of photography on paper. The subject matter of these photographers centered on family, friends, and the landscape adjacent to their country estates. Favorite animals were treated as family and proudly recorded in photographs. *Sultan* is an unusually candid photograph for this early period of photography. It is an entertaining image from the photographer's personal collection in which the portrait of the horse clearly takes precedence over that of his diminutive human mistress.

5. Photographer unknown. *The Farrier.* 1848–50. Sixth-plate daguerreotype. Collection Matthew Isenberg

Among the specialties of blacksmithing is the profession of the farrier, or horseshoer. The first authoritative evidence of a nailed-on metal horseshoe was found in the tomb of the French knight Childeric about A.D. 481. Ancient nomads had ridden unshod horses over the desert, and the Tartars, Kalmucks, and Turks had used rawhide coverings. With the advent of paved roads and the systematic stabling and pasturing of horses, ironically their hooves needed protection from increasingly civilized environments. The Greeks and Romans devised metal-plated leather boots, often decorated with gold and silver trim. Sixteenth-century Spanish explorers in America, lacking sources for iron, had to use silver. Proving to be too soft, silver was replaced by the old rawhide method, a tradition passed on to the American Indian. Mythological and religious legend has always associated the horseshoe with good fortune. A daguerreotype of a horse being shod is unusual because of the long exposure required and the volatility of the animal.

6. J. Newman. Dates unknown. *Polo Pony.* c. 1850. Half-plate daguerreotype. Collection Charles Schwartz

The polo pony is not a specific breed, nor does it necessarily conform to the size classification of a pony. Instead, the horse must be uniquely trained and of a size dictated by that of the rider. Although the American quarter horse is frequently used, the influence of the Arab and the Barb is strongly apparent. Whatever breed is used, the animal must have vigorous hindquarters for quick acceleration and forelegs capable of abrupt turns and rapid stops. The horse must be acutely sensitive to the touch of the bit, to nuances of leg pressure, and to manipulation of the reins. Add agility, balance, a gentle trot, calm temperament, and stamina to the requirements, and it is clearly a demanding task to find the required twelve to sixteen horses needed to equip a polo team. Nothing is known about the photographer of this early example of sporting photography, except that the metal mat enclosing the daguerreotype is stamped "J. Newman, Artist."

7. Jean-Gabriel Eynard-Lullin and Jean Rion. Eynard-Lullin, Swiss, 1775–1863; Rion, dates unknown. *M. Eynard, Griselda, Félix.* c. 1843–52. Full-plate daguerreotype. International Museum of Photography at George Eastman House, Rochester, New York

A true Renaissance man, Eynard spent his early career as a banker in Italy, belonged to various societies for the arts and literature, and pursued international politics. After the announcement of photography in 1839, he became interested in the new medium and began making daguerreotypes in Switzerland, France, and Greece. Works such as this handsomely composed self-portrait in a carriage pulled by his horse, Griselda, received praise in contemporary photography circles.

8. Mayer & Pierson (Héribert Mayer and Louis Pierson). Active Paris, 1850s–60s. *The Prince Imperial on His Pony Being Photographed.* c. 1859. Albumen print from wet collodion-on-glass negative, 6⅝ × 6⅝″. Collection Gérard Lévy and François LePage, Paris

Mayer and Pierson photographed the Prince Imperial, son of Emperor Napoleon III, seated on his pony, Bouton d'Or. In this uncropped version of the portrait, the two- or three-year-old prince was flanked on the right by his father and on the left by the equerry Bachon. The cabinet-card version of the image, perhaps intended to be sold commercially, was trimmed so that it showed only the prince, rigidly frontal and strapped onto his thronelike saddle. The official air of the trimmed portrait belies the notion of a boy's childhood adventures with his pony, while the uncut image suggests the casual and spontaneous atmosphere in a photographic studio, even when the subject was royalty. Mayer and Pierson operated a portrait studio and are remembered especially for their ubiquitous cartes-de-visite, the photographic calling card of the nineteenth century.

9. Photographer unknown. Untitled. 1870s. Albumen print from wet collodion-on-glass negative, 8⅛ × 6″. Courtesy The Tartt Gallery, Washington, D.C.

The rocking horse was a familiar prop in nineteenth-century portraits of children, especially boys. An anonymous photographer has captured this particularly imperious little boy, his hand resting possessively on the horse's head. The presence of the horse in the image suggests an amusing child's version of the "mounted emperor" school of sculpture.

10. Adrien Tournachon. French, 1825–1903. *Mouton.* c. 1855. From *Races Chevaline et Asine, Primés à l'Exposition de 1855.* Albumen print from paper negative, 6⅞ × 8⅞″. International Museum of Photography at George Eastman House, Rochester, New York

At the urging of his brother, Nadar, Adrien Tournachon took up photography in 1854, initially studying with Gustave Le Gray. The two brothers had a brief and stormy collaboration, and ultimately a lawsuit brought against him by Nadar enjoined Tournachon from signing his prints with the pseudonym "Nadar Jeune." He continued to operate a studio, and in 1854 he made a compelling series of portraits of the mime Charles Deburau. Tournachon's talent for portraiture extended to elegant views of prize livestock and horses such as Mouton; he often organized such work into beautiful presentation albums. With the growing popularity of horseback riding in Paris, he opened an equestrian annex on the avenue des Champs-Elysées.

11. GEORGE FRANCIS SCHREIBER. American, born Germany, 1803–1892. Untitled. c. 1881. Platinum print, handcolored, 19⅝ × 27½″. International Museum of Photography at George Eastman House, Rochester, New York

When the printer George Francis Schreiber arrived in Philadelphia in 1834, he initially published a German newspaper. When he became interested in photography, he sold the paper and entered into a silent partnership with the camera-manufacturing firm of William and Frederick Langenheim. A pioneer photographer, Schreiber started his career as a daguerreotypist of human subjects. Eventually, he opened the firm of Schreiber and Sons and began dedicating himself solely to the photography on paper of domestic animals, for which he is renowned. His *Studies from Nature* depicted notable horses, cattle, dogs, and fancy fowls. In 1873 Schreiber published *Schreiber and Sons Portraits of Noted Horses of America*, the first photographic book of its kind to depict the trotters and Thoroughbreds whose names and bloodlines live on in today's famous racehorses. Among his subjects were Hambletonian, the founding sire of the Standard Breed of the trotting horse, and Lexington, the great and potent American Thoroughbred. Schreiber's success contributed greatly to the decline of the nineteenth-century animal portrait painter.

12. JULIA MARGARET CAMERON (attributed). Engish, 1815–1879. *The Bowden-Smiths at Darley House, Colombo, Ceylon*. 1873. Albumen print from wet collodion-on-glass negative, 5⅜ × 7⅞″. Gilman Paper Company Collection

In 1875, the celebrated Victorian photographer Julia Margaret Cameron and her husband, Charles, left England and returned to their former expatriate life in India. The photographer had been born in Calcutta in 1815 and had married Charles Hay Cameron in 1834, while he was serving the British Empire as a member of the Council of Calcutta. The Camerons spent their last years in Ceylon, where their sons lived and where Charles had cultivated his beloved coffee plantations. Cameron died in 1879, and her husband the following year. Lou Bowden-Smith was the niece of Cameron's sister, Sarah Prinsep. From an album presented by the photographer to her son, Henry Hay Cameron, this family photograph depicts Lou seated sidesaddle on her horse, Lowood.

13. C. FAMIN. French, active 1860s–70s. *Horse*. c. 1874. Albumen print from wet collodion-on-glass negative, 6⅛ × 4¾″. Bibliothèque Nationale, Paris

Although Famin remains an obscure figure in early French photography, it is known that he had a studio in Paris and produced landscape and rural farm studies presumably as an aid to painters—a tradition that Atget perpetuated into the twentieth century. Famin's photograph of the white horse is unusual in its lighting and vantage point. In an era when horses were customarily photographed in profile and stillness was rigorously sought, Famin has seized the opportunity in the horse's unwanted movement and has created a spontaneous-looking, and some have suggested Impressionistic, view of the animal's hindquarters.

14. NADAR (Gaspard-Félix Tournachon). French, 1820–1910. Untitled. c. 1865. Albumen print from wet collodion-on-glass negative, 8 × 9¾″. Courtesy Charles Isaacs, Malvern, Pennsylvania

Nadar, a journalist and caricaturist, opened his photographic portrait studio in 1854 and began to record the artists and intellectuals of Parisian society. His attraction to photography undoubtedly stemmed from his project, begun in 1853, of creating lithographic caricatures of the thousand most well known faces of the day, his "Panthéon-Nadar." Nadar was a dynamic personality with a gift for self-promotion. His studio became a meeting place for prominent personalities, and in 1874 it was the site of the first Impressionist exhibition. This elegant portrait of the man on horseback relates to the work of Nadar's younger brother, Adrien Tournachon (plate 10), known for his photographs of racehorses and prize animals at the agricultural fairs of 1855 and 1860. It is also interesting to note that the same painted backdrop appears in photographs made by Nadar's contemporary the equestrian photographer Louis-Jean Delton (plate 35). However, a variant of this portrait bears Nadar's blindstamp, and the fashionable and commercial character of the image clearly indicates his authorship.

15. ROGER FENTON. English, 1819–1869. *Lieutenant General Barnard's Horse, Grandson of Marengo*. 1855. Salt print from wet collodion-on-glass negative, 6 × 5⅞″. Courtesy Robert Hershkowitz Ltd., London

Fenton spent four months in 1855 photographing the Russo-Turkish War in the Crimea. He had been commissioned by the art dealer and publisher T. Agnew & Sons to record, in portraits, camp scenes, and landscapes, not the horrors of war but rather images that would reassure the uneasy British public that their troops were not suffering or dying unnecessarily. Fenton made a series of portraits on horseback, among them this stately example featuring a horse with a most distinguished grandfather. The stallion Marengo was Napoleon Bonaparte's favorite among his more than sixty white horses. Named in honor of the victory of the French cavalry over the Austrians at the Battle of Marengo, this horse carried Napoleon for eight hours in his final defeat at the Battle of Waterloo. Marengo was subsequently purchased by a Frenchman and spent the last of his thirty-six years on an English estate in Kent. He died in 1829, outliving Napoleon by eight years.

16. GUSTAVE LE GRAY. French, 1820–1882. *The Camp at Châlons, Maneuvers of October* 3, *1857*. Albumen print from wet collodion-on-glass negative, 11⅛ × 14⅜″. Bibliothèque Nationale, Paris

In 1857, Le Gray was commissioned by Napoleon III to photograph the newly created military camp near Châlons-sur-Marne, east of Paris. His depictions of the maneuvers, the imperial pavilions, and camp life were later bound in albums and presented to the emperor's general officers and special admirers. This image portrays the final *grande manoeuvre*—a hypothetical and carefully choreographed battle against an imaginary enemy—from the inaugural series of exercises, involving a total of 21,365 men and 5,871 horses over a period of more than a month. The earthen breastwork was the protective centerpiece for the battle of October 3, and in Le Gray's photograph, it was occupied by the grenadiers and reinforced by cavalry officers. By operating at a distance, Le Gray overcame the technical limitations on the camera's ability to stop action and created an image of great beauty.

17. MICHAEL MILEY. American, 1841–1918. *General Robert E. Lee on Traveller*. 1868. Albumen print from wet collodion-on-glass negative, 6⅜ × 8⅞″. Eleanor S. Brockenbrough Library, The Museum of the Confederacy, Richmond, Virginia

The horse of a commanding officer was often as well known to the public as the man himself, and the soldiers in his command frequently shared this strong emotional attachment to the animal. The "iron gray" general and horse—Stephen Vincent Benet's apt description of General Robert E. Lee and Traveller—were symbols to the Confederate army. Traveller carried Lee in the Battle of the Wilderness and the second Battle of Bull Run, saving his master's life at least once in the course of the Civil War. Lee rode Traveller to Appomattox in April 1865, when he met with General Ulysses S. Grant to arrange for the Confederate surrender. After the war, when Lee came to Lexington, Virginia, to become president of Washington College, he asked a newfound friend, photographer Michael Miley, to make this portrait in his uniform and mounted on Traveller, "just as we went through the four years of war together." It was the great general's first and only request to be photographed in a Confederate uniform. In 1870, Traveller followed the hearse in his master's funeral procession. Two years later, the war-horse died of lockjaw after stepping on a rusty nail in his pasture.

18. ANDREW J. RUSSELL. American, 1830–1902. *Rebel Caisson Destroyed by Federal Shells, at Fredericksburg, May* 3, *1863*. Albumen print from wet collodion-on-glass negative, 9 × 12¾″. Courtesy Janet Lehr, Inc., New York

Captain Andrew Joseph Russell had the rare distinction of being an official army photographer during the Civil War, rather than operating under the auspices of a commercial studio. Russell enlisted in 1862 and was sent to Washington, D.C., with the 141st New York Volunteers. The following year, he was assigned to the U.S. Military Railroad Construction Corps, which was active in Virginia. He chronicled the engineering developments of the railroad as well as the battlefields, camps, and gunboats around Fredericksburg, Petersburg, Brandy, and Alexandria, and finally the ruins of Richmond. Russell's photographs became a historical record and a guide for units stationed elsewhere. His image of the ruined rebel caisson is a poignant reminder of the countless equine casualties in the last great war fought on horseback.

19. ALEXANDER GARDNER. American, born Scotland, 1821–1882. *Dead Horse of a Confederate Colonel, Near the East Woods, on or About September* 20, *1862*. Stereo view, albumen print from wet collodion-on-glass negative. Library of Congress, Washington, D.C.

General Robert E. Lee's campaign to drive the Civil War northward by invading Maryland culminated in the Battle of Antietam. The efforts of his Army of Northern Virginia were ultimately thwarted by General George B. McClellan's Union forces, but not before death or injury had come to 26,000 Confederate and Union soldiers, making September 17, 1862, the bloodiest day in American history. Gardner and his assistant, James F. Gibson, photographed the aftermath of the siege, beginning their work about September 19, only hours after the Confederates had withdrawn from the field. Among the carnage, they found the body of this hauntingly lifelike horse killed in the conflict. According to his journals, Oliver Wendell Holmes also saw this horse while he was combing the area in an eventually successful search for his son and namesake, reportedly wounded in the battle.

20. TIMOTHY O'SULLIVAN. American, born Ireland, 1840–1882. *The Halt*. 1864. Plate from Gardner's *Photographic Sketchbook of the War* (1866). Albumen print from wet collodion-on-glass negative (negative made by O'Sullivan, printed by Alexander Gardner), 6¾ × 8⅞″. National Gallery of Canada, Ottawa

O'Sullivan contributed nearly half of the hundred photographs in Gardner's monumental publication documenting the American Civil War. According to Civil War scholars, the horse in this image was of the highest calibre, sought in the Northern states to outfit the staff and regimental officers of the Union armies. The animal's admiring master was Captain Harry Page, quartermaster of the Headquarters of the Army of the Potomac and subsequently colonel and chief quartermaster of the cavalry corps under General Philip Sheridan. Page had apparently just ridden forward to inspect the campsite shown and was awaiting the wagon train. The image is a compelling portrait of the relationship between two partners in war. While many of O'Sullivan's other photographs in the *Sketchbook* depicted corpse-strewn battlefields and the aftermath of war, *The Halt* reveals a quiet, personal moment of pleasure.

21. DAVID KNOX. American, active 1860s. *Forge Scene, Front of Petersburg, August, 1864*. Plate from Gardner's *Photographic Sketchbook of the War* (1866). Albumen print from wet collodion-on-glass negative (negative made by Knox, printed by Alexander Gardner), 6⅞ × 8⅞″. Courtesy National Archives, Washington, D.C., Photo Number 165-SB-77

Little is known about Knox except that he was part of Mathew Brady's staff and became one of the more active field photographers in the eastern arena of the Civil War during Grant's last campaign. Knox contributed four photographs to Gardner's monumental publication documenting the war. The two-volume *Sketchbook* presented many of the finest photographers of the day, but was an otherwise unsuccessful commercial venture in a country embittered by war. Knox tended to portray domestic camp scenes like this view of an army forge. The forge represented a hub of activity in camps that sprang up around battlesites throughout the South. The blacksmith was as important as a doctor, for he serviced the indispensable horses who hauled the supplies and carried the soldiers in battle.

22. MATHEW B. BRADY. American, 1823–1896. *General Rawlins's Horse; Taken at Cold Harbor, Virginia, June 14, 1864*. Stereo view (Brady & Co., no. 2431), albumen print from wet collodion-on-glass negative. Collection Charles Schwartz

Brady began his career in photography as a daguerreotypist,

learning his trade from the famous inventor and artist Samuel F. B. Morse. By 1854, he had shifted to the faster and more versatile process of collodion, which the photographers in his New York and Washington galleries would use to assemble the Brady & Co. documentation of the Civil War. Failing eyesight and administrative responsibilities precluded Brady from taking many of the photographs bearing his company's imprint; instead, these images were made by employees such as Timothy O'Sullivan, Alexander Gardner, and George Barnard, who later went on to establish their own important reputations. It was undoubtedly one of the Brady photographers who captured this poignant image of a small Black stable boy exercising the horse of General John Aaron Rawlins, the Federal Brigadier-general of volunteers. Rawlins was later promoted in rank for his brave and meritorious services during the campaign that ultimately brought about the surrender of the Confederate army under General Robert E. Lee.

23. Photographer unknown. *The Horse Drawing*. 1870s. Two sixth-plate tintypes. Collection Martin Weinstein

The tintype was a uniquely American innovation, patented in 1856 by Hamilton L. Smith, professor of natural science at Kenyon College in Ohio. Like a daguerreotype, the tintype is one of a kind, but it is made by a far less expensive process, involving simply the exposed collodion emulsion resting on a support of black japanned iron. This rugged form of photography was ideal for campaign buttons in the 1860 presidential campaign, and during the Civil War, young soldiers had themselves photographed by itinerant tintypists for souvenirs to be sent home to friends and family. These paired tintypes depicting a horse drawing are a curiously sophisticated use of a still-primitive medium. The two men, maybe brothers, seem to be displaying pride of ownership—perhaps one is the creator of the drawing, or they are indicating with their pointing gesture that they are the proud owners of a handsome horse. In their naive manipulation of reality, the tintypes suggest a Conceptual approach to art, or expression, that would prevail a century later.

24. FRANK B. FISKE. American, 1883–1952. *Tipis, Standing Rock Indian Reservation*. n.d. Silver print, 4½ × 6⅝". State Historical Society of North Dakota, Bismarck

Fiske was part of the second generation of Western landscape photographers, following after Carleton Watkins, Timothy O'Sullivan, and Eadweard Muybridge. Although he is known to have photographed in Yosemite, he spent most of his life operating various photography studios in the Fort Yates area of North Dakota. Fiske recorded the life and landscape of central and southern North Dakota in over seven thousand images. Best remembered for his Indian portraits, especially of the Standing Rock Sioux, he made this image of the Sioux teepees at Fort Yates, a site for Indian relocation. The scenes on the teepees, identified as One Bull's (*left*) and Old Bull's (*right*), depict casualties counted during the Battle of the Little Big Horn, in which Sitting Bull's forces defeated Civil War General George Armstrong Custer and his 265 soldiers of the United States Seventh Cavalry.

25. D. F. BARRY. American, died 1934. *Comanche*. 1870s. Cabinet card, albumen print from wet collodion-on-glass negative, 4 × 6". Courtesy Montana Historical Society, Helena

The mysterious sole survivor of General George Armstrong Custer's forces in his battle with the Sioux at the Little Big Horn, Montana, on June 25, 1876, was a horse named Comanche. He was found on the battlefield, two days after the massacre, with a deep wound in his neck and dragging his reins. The true story of the victory of Crazy Horse, Chief Galls, and Rain-in-the-Face was known only to this wounded mount, ridden by Captain Myles W. Keogh. Comanche had been a veteran of cavalry action, earning his name from a wound in his right quarter inflicted by a Comanche flint-point arrow. After the Little Big Horn, he lived in honored retirement, never ridden or worked. His sole duty was to participate in ceremonies and parades, in which he always appeared riderless and draped in mourning, reversed boots in his stirrups. He died of colic on November 6, 1891. The photographer D. F. Barry operated a studio in Bismarck, Dakota Territory, and specialized in ethnographic and military subjects.

26. EDWARD S. CURTIS. American, 1868–1952. *A Painted Tipi—Assiniboin*. 1926. Plate 633 from *The North American Indian*, 1907–30. Photogravure, 11⅜ × 15¾". Library of Congress, Washington, D.C.

From 1900 to 1930, Curtis produced his monumental work, *The North American Indian*. The complete set contained twenty volumes of text with 1,505 photogravures accompanied by twenty folios of 715 large-format photogravures. Curtis initially funded the project himself, but in 1906, with the support of President Theodore Roosevelt, he was able to win the much-needed sponsorship of J. P. Morgan, whose family continued the financial commitment even after the financier's death in 1913. Curtis lived with the Indian peoples he photographed. In addition to recording their customs, he made portraits such as this one of a young child astride the handsome Medicine Hat Horse. Although a breed of small horses existed on the North American continent thousands of years ago, some force in nature caused its extinction. When the Spanish explorers reintroduced the horse in the sixteenth century, the Indians were both frightened and fascinated. It was not long, however, before they discovered the advantages of the animal for transport, hunting, war, and work. The Indians became active breeders by necessity, for whether farmers or hunters, they came to depend on the horse for their very existence. Curtis's portrait strongly reflects this bond.

27. ELIZABETH ROBERTS. American, 1873–1968. *Frank Roberts With Horse Tied, Slope County, N.D.* c. 1910. Silver print, 7⅜ × 7⅜". State Historical Society of North Dakota, Bismarck

An avid horsewoman and protector of wildlife, Roberts was North Dakota's first woman game warden. She served in that capacity for thirty years. She and her husband, Frank, operated the Bull Head Ranch and raised registered Percheron horses. *Frank Roberts With Horse Tied* is part of a large collection of Roberts's photographs depicting ranch life at the turn of the century. The rodeo has been seen as a metaphor for the taming of the West, and this image of the tightly bound and helpless horse further suggests man's need to control nature.

28. Photographer unknown. *Jesse James on Horseback*. c. 1870. Tintype, 2⅝ × 3¼". Everhard Collection, Amon Carter Museum, Fort Worth, Texas

The sons of Reverend Robert James, Frank and Jesse, were hardened by the Civil War and the bloody border wars between Missouri and Kansas. Expert horseback riders, crack shots, and fearless young outlaws, they teamed up with Cole Younger and his brothers to form the James-Younger Gang, the most ruthless and enduring of the legendary outlaws of the Wild West. In 1866, about four years before Jesse was memorialized in this anonymous tintype, he led the gang in its first bank robbery in Liberty, Missouri; he was hardly nineteen years of age. For the next ten years, the James-Younger Gang carried on a spree of crime that ended with the famous shootout at the First National Bank in Northfield, Minnesota. Frank and Jesse escaped to Mexico or South America. In 1882, after resurfacing briefly with a new gang, Jesse was assassinated by one of his own men, who had made a deal with the governor of Missouri. This small tintype of Jesse James seated on his faithful steed and wielding his gun evokes some of the romance of the Wild West.

29. LATON A. HUFFMAN. American, 1854–1931. *Andy Speelman, Ekalaka, Saddling a Wild Horse*. 1894. Collotype, 10 × 8". Courtesy Ezra Mack, New York

In 1878, two years after Custer's defeat at the Little Big Horn and one year after the surrender of Chief Joseph, Huffman arrived at Fort Keogh, Montana Territory, to assume the position of post photographer. He had learned his trade from F. J. Haynes, the longtime official photographer of Yellowstone National Park. Huffman traveled throughout the Montana Territory, documenting all aspects of the taming of the Wild West: the suppression of the Indians, the disappearing herds of bison, the cowboys and cattle roundups, and the building of the railroad. It is said that upon seeing Huffman's photograph of Andy Speelman, one rancher commented respectfully on the cowboy's ability to saddle this unbroken horse without the aid of a corral or the protection of leather chaps. Equally amazing was Huffman's skill in capturing this dramatic moment.

30. FRANK JAY HAYNES. American, 1853–1921. *Iron Car Horse "Nig" at Last Spike, Villard Excursion, Sept. 8, 1883*. Albumen print from wet collodion-on-glass negative, 6⅝" × 9⅞". Haynes Foundation Collection, Montana Historical Society, Helena

For thirty-two years, beginning with his appointment in 1884, Haynes was the official photographer of Yellowstone National Park (Mount Haynes commemorates his work there). From 1881 to 1902, he also held the position of official photographer for the Northern Pacific Railway. His photograph of Nig, made for the Northern Pacific, portrays the horse who had drawn the iron car 750 miles. The massive engineering feat of building the railroad, which would ultimately replace the horse, would have been impossible to accomplish without the animal's help in hauling men, machinery, and materials.

31. GIUSEPPE PRIMOLI. Italian, 1851–1927. *Annie Oakley, Rome, March 1890*. Silver print, 7 × 4¾". Fondazione Giuseppe Primoli, Rome

Annie Oakley, known as Little Sure Shot, was twenty-five years of age when she joined Buffalo Bill's Wild West Show in 1885. For already half her life, she had been honing her skills with the rifle, shotgun, and six-gun. Whether firing at glass balls while on the back of a galloping horse or shooting a cigarette out of the mouth of the future Kaiser Wilhelm II, Annie never missed. For seventeen years, she was the first act in Buffalo Bill's traveling show, and she performed during the troupe's three trips to Europe between 1887 and 1906. During the engagement in Rome in 1890, photographer Giuseppe Primoli, notorious chronicler of high and low society, made this lively image of the amazing Annie.

32. Photographer unknown. *Buffalo Bill*. c. 1887. Stereo view, albumen print from wet collodion-on-glass negative. Buffalo Bill Historical Center, Cody, Wyoming.

William F. Cody had various careers as Indian scout and fighter, buffalo hunter, actor, and finally star of his own "Wild West" show. The stallions Old Charlie and Buckskin Joe and the Indian ponies Tall Bull and Brigham carried Cody on many of his early adventures. In his later years, he rode white mounts and dressed in fringed and beaded buckskin with a white Stetson. The artist Rosa Bonheur painted him in such garb when his show toured Europe in 1889. He died in 1917. Seen through a stereo viewer, this early example of a moving subject displays a cinematic effect.

33. EADWEARD MUYBRIDGE. American, born England, 1830–1904. Plate 640 from *Animal Locomotion*. 1887. Collotype, 9⅞ × 12". The Minneapolis Institute of Arts

In 1887, Muybridge published his monumental work, *Animal Locomotion*, eleven volumes containing 781 collotypes that reproduced over twenty thousand separate exposures of human beings, animals, and birds in various stages of motion. It was the culmination of the now-celebrated challenge made to Muybridge in 1872 by Leland Stanford to determine through photography whether all four feet of a horse, when moving at top speed, ever left the ground at the same time. Six years later, the photographer finally succeeded in clearly recording the sequences of a horse's motion and confirmed Stanford's speculation that they did. However, Muybridge's conclusions completely upset the conventions of portraying horses in painting, from ancient eras to the contemporary work of Edgar Degas and Jean Meissonier. He found that, at full gallop, the horse's feet are gathered under the belly rather than in the extended "rocking-horse" style previously supposed. Muybridge's studies were the foundation for further experiments and developments in the photography of motion.

34. ETIENNE-JULES MAREY. French, 1830–1904. *Cheval au Trot*. 1886. Albumen print, 5½ × 9⅛". Cinémathèque Française, Paris

Inspired by Muybridge's work on the photography of motion, the physiologist Etienne-Jules Marey experimented with a technique in which several cameras could be arranged to record a sequence of images on a single plate. In 1887, his work culminated in the invention of the chronophotographic camera, which could record long series of action images on rolls of light-sensitized material. Revolutionary in its technical achievement, this portrayal of the fluid motion of a trotting horse anticipated the imagery of the Italian Futurist artists more than twenty years later.

35. LOUIS-JEAN DELTON. Before 1820–after 1896. *Woman on Horseback, Taking a Jump*. 1884. From *Le Tour du Bois* (Paris, 1884). Albumen prints from glass-plate negatives, each 4⅛ × 3¾″. Bibliothèque Nationale, Paris

Listed as a member of the Jockey Club in 1835, Delton was esteemed throughout Europe for his photographs of equestrians, jockeys, and racehorses. Between 1889 and 1894, he edited the periodical *La Photographie hippique*, in which this early motion study of a woman on horseback appears. The reconstruction of Paris, begun in 1849, created grand boulevards and spacious city parks where Parisians were encouraged to congregate and amuse themselves. The Champs-Elysées became a fashionable promenade for equestrians, and photographers' ministudios were established in the Bois de Boulogne to record the new social rituals of the French middle class.

36. C. REID. English, active 1860s–80s. Untitled. 1880s. Albumen print from wet collodion-on-glass negative, 4½ × 7⅛″. Private collection, New York

The oldest surviving sport on horseback, the English fox hunt has met with its share of criticism: Oscar Wilde once characterized it as "the unspeakable in full pursuit of the uneatable." Yet the hunt is still practiced with particular vigor in English-speaking countries, using the same etiquette that was established centuries ago. The United States and Canada have about 140 hunts a year, and in the state of Virginia alone, there are 20. The hunt is governed by the Master, assisted by a Field Master, who controls the hunt-followers, or field. The Huntsman manages the pack of forty or more hounds and is assisted by one or two Whippers-in, who retrieve stray hounds and generally keep the pack on course. When the hounds have discovered and taken up the scent, the field follows, always careful not to overtake the Master and the pack. Little is known about the maker of this image except that he specialized in genre subjects. His photograph of the hunt suggests the eighteenth- and nineteenth-century tradition of the English sporting print.

37. Photographer unknown. Untitled. 1860s. Carte-de-visite, albumen prints from wet collodion-on-glass negatives. Courtesy Keith de Lellis Fine Arts, New York

The carte-de-visite was patented by Parisian photographer André-Adolphe-Eugène Disdéri in 1854. Disdéri discovered a technique for the inexpensive mass production of photographs by exposing multiple images on a single wet-collodion plate. The size of a 4-by-2½-inch visiting card, the carte became the rage as everyone began collecting these tiny portraits of family and celebrities and assembling them in albums. Photography studios competed with one another for the opportunity of photographing and distributing cartes of the famous and infamous. Although the production of cartes-de-visite continued into the 1880s, their popularity gradually declined with the introduction of the cabinet card in 1866. In addition to portraits, cartes-de-visite eventually depicted topographical and genre subjects as well as sporting images like this assemblage of prominent racehorses by an unknown French or English photography studio. This carte contains individual copy prints of photographs probably made by various photographers; it is known that the central image of "The Ranger" was made by Louis-Jean Delton, a popular equestrian photographer in Paris (plate 35).

38. PETER HENRY EMERSON. English, born Cuba, 1856–1936. *The Clay-Mill (Norfolk)*. Before 1888. From *Pictures of East Anglian Life* (London, 1888). Photogravure, 7⅞ × 11⅜″. National Gallery of Canada, Ottawa

39. PETER HENRY EMERSON. *A Stiff Pull*. Before 1888. From *Pictures of East Anglian Life* (London, 1888). Photogravure, 8⅛ × 11¼″. National Gallery of Canada, Ottawa

Pictures of East Anglian Life was the fourth of eight books and portfolios of photographs that Emerson would produce in the decade between 1886 and 1895. Champion of naturalistic photography and vehement opponent of the "high-art," painting-inspired photographer, he set out as an anthropologist would to document the life and work of the peasants of East Anglia. His photographs of laborers and their horse toiling at a clay mill and of a farmer urging his plowhorses onward are celebrations of preindustrial life in a world that was

becoming increasingly mechanized. In Emerson's straightforward narratives, the horse symbolized the very essence of the life and trade of a rural peasant society.

40. FRANK M. SUTCLIFFE. English, 1853–1941. Untitled. 1870s. Albumen print from wet collodion-on-glass negative, 5¼ × 7¾″. Collection Richard and Ronay Menschel

Sutcliffe portrayed the traditional, picturesque aspects of life at Whitby, a village on the northern coast of Yorkshire where fishing and boat-building industries were gradually yielding to mechanization and to the tourist trade. In season, he made his living by tourist portraiture, but the noncommercial work for which he is most known focused lovingly on Whitby's fishermen and artisans and their families at work and play. Sutcliffe advocated the "truth to nature" philosophy of The Linked Ring, a group devoted to the promotion of art photography. A purist and naturalist, he created straightforward images such as this rustic scene of horses on the beach. Horses were often seen on the beach at Whitby pulling carts of coal that had been offloaded from incoming ships.

41. CARLO PONTI. Italian, active 1858–1875. *Horses of Saint Mark's, Venice*. c. 1860. Albumen print from wet collodion-on-glass negative, 10¾ × 13½″. Collection Richard and Ronay Menschel

Ponti operated a shop on the Piazza San Marco in which he sold fine lenses and his own photographic views of Venice and other Italian cities. With the unification of Venice and Italy in 1866, he became optician and photographer to King Victor Emmanuel II. One of his signature images of Venice portrays the celebrated golden horses on the loggia of Saint Mark's Cathedral. In the fourteenth century, when the Genoese spoke of defeating their archenemies, the Venetians, they declared that they would "bridle the proud horses of San Marco." Of Greek origin, the horses were brought to Venice from Constantinople in 1204 as trophies of war. They were believed to be bronze until they were examined and restored in the 1970s and were found to be copper with parcel gilding. Today, bronze copies stand on the church loggia, and the original horses are on display in a small room of Saint Mark's.

42. WALTER HEGE. German, 1893–1955. *Rearing Horse—West Frieze, Parthenon*. c. 1928. Silver print, 11⅜ × 8¾″. The Art Institute of Chicago, Julien Levy Collection, gift of Jean and Julien Levy, 1978.1068

After teaching himself photography, Hege studied for two years with the well-known German photographer Hugo Erfurth. In 1922, he opened a studio in Naumburg and began photographing and publishing books on German architectural monuments. The Metropolitan Museum of Art in New York learned of his work and commissioned him to photograph Greek sculpture and architecture in Athens; the two-year project culminated in the publication of *Die Akropolis* in 1929. For the project, Hege invented a unique exposure/development/printing procedure that eliminated strong contrasts and revealed detail ordinarily obscured in shadow. In isolating this detail from an equestrian frieze on the Parthenon, he has used his special technique to make the straining of the horse nearly palpable.

43. W. A. MANSELL & CO. English studio, photographs dated 1860s–1870s. *Panel From Parthenon Frieze*. 1860s. Albumen print from wet collodion-on-glass negative, 9¼ × 8⅛″. Collection Gordon L. Bennett

Mythological creatures of pre-Homeric origin, centaurs were half human, half horse and lived on the wooded mountains of Thessaly. With the exception of the wise and beneficent Chiron, these beasts personified such primitive traits as inebriation, lasciviousness, and belligerence. The Mansell photograph depicts the centaurs' mischievous nature in a scene from their legendary battle with the Lapiths at the marriage of Hippodamia with the Lapith king, Pirithoüs. The fragment in the photograph is a part of the group of stone sculptures removed from the Parthenon by the seventh Earl of Elgin in 1801–3, when he was ambassador to Turkey. Considered the finest surviving examples of the work of Phidias, the Elgin Marbles are at present in the collection of the British Museum; their ownership is a subject of ongoing controversy.

44. CHARLES NÈGRE. French, 1820–1880. *Fame Riding Pegasus, Tuileries Gardens, Paris*. 1859. Albumen print from wet collodion-on-glass negative, 17½ × 14″. Musée d'Orsay, Paris. Gift of Joseph Nègre, 1981

A student of painting with Delaroche and Ingres, Nègre initially became involved in photography in 1844 as an aid to his genre painting. His reputation as a photographer grew, and he received numerous government commissions. Napoleon III was a great patron of photography and often used it as a propaganda tool to glorify the activities of his regime. In 1859, the emperor commissioned Nègre to make a series of photographs depicting the sculptures of the Tuileries Gardens. *Fame Riding Pegasus* is the work of the seventeenth-century French sculptor Antoine Coysevox who, in the employ of Charles Le Brun, also made the equestrian relief of Louis XIV in the Salon de la Guerre at Versailles.

45. EUGÈNE ATGET. French, 1857–1927. *Luxembourg, Fontaine Carpeaux*. 1901–2. Albumen print from glass-plate negative, 9⅜ × 7″. The Museum of Modern Art, New York. Abbott-Levy Collection. Partial gift of Shirley C. Burden

At the age of forty, after various careers as a merchant seaman, actor, and painter, Atget turned to photography and spent the rest of his life making what he called "documents" of the city of Paris and its environs. In this image, a humorous tone underlies the magnificent vista of the Avenue de l'Observatoire and the beauty of the reflections in the water. Instead of depicting the entire fountain, a monumental work with teams of rearing horses and metaphorical figures of the four continents supporting a spherical model of the universe, Atget chose to focus on the small vignette of a spirited dialogue between horse and turtle. The animals in the fountain were made by the noted nineteenth-century animal sculptor Emmanuel Frémiet.

46. ALVIN LANGDON COBURN. British, born America, 1882–1966. *Trevi Fountain, Rome*. 1906. Gum bichromate/platinum print, 11½ × 14⅜″. International Museum of Photography at George Eastman House, Rochester, New York

Acquiring his first camera at the age of eight, Coburn received early encouragement from his distant cousin, the photographer F. Holland Day. By the time he was twenty-one, he had achieved success as a founding member of the Photo-Secession in America and as an elected member of an important related organization in England, The Linked Ring. During the summers of 1902 and 1903, Coburn studied with Arthur Wesley Dow, the preeminent art teacher in America, who introduced the young photographer to the influences of *japonisme*. In *Trevi Fountain*, Coburn used elements characteristic of Japanese wood-block prints such as asymmetry, shallow spatial relationships, and dramatically graphic light and dark effects. During the same period, Coburn was also exploring aspects of the Symbolist movement in art and literature. To suggest the correspondence between the physical and spiritual worlds, the basis of Symbolist theory, he frequently used a soft-focus lens, as he does here in his photograph of the now-tourist-worn Baroque fountain. A vision of Neptune driving his chariot of horses, the fountain is mainly the work of Nicolo Salvi and was completed in the mid-eighteenth century.

47. FRANK EUGENE. American, 1865–1936. *Horse*. 1895. From *Camera Work*, no. 30 (April 1910). Photogravure, 4⅛ × 8⅛″. Philadelphia Museum of Art: From the Collection of Dorothy Norman

An accomplished portrait painter, Eugene took up photography as a hobby in 1885. His membership in the New York Camera Club brought him to Alfred Stieglitz's attention, and by 1902 he was one of the twelve founding members of Stieglitz's Photo-Secessionist movement, a group of photographers devoted to the promotion of photography as a fine art. Eugene's origins in painting profoundly influenced his photography; his manipulation of the negative by etching or painting typically produced a print that hardly resembled a photograph. Although this image was probably made outdoors or in a stable, Eugene has obliterated the background by etching the negative, and the animal is vignetted in a mysterious, undefined space.

48. GEORGE SEELEY. American, 1880–1955. *Youth With Horse*, c. 1907. Platinum print, 9½ × 7⅝″. Library of Congress, Washington, D.C.

Seeley spent his entire reclusive life in Stockbridge, Massachusetts, insulated from the vicissitudes of life by family and a few friends. Alfred Stieglitz saw his work exhibited in New York in Curtis Bell's First American Salon of 1904 and invited him to join the Photo-Secessionist group. A reluctant joiner, Seeley delayed his acceptance until 1906 and his first meeting with Stieglitz until 1908. The allegorical *Youth With Horse* suggests the influence of photographer F. Holland Day, an eccentric himself and one of the few photographers with whom Seeley had a lasting friendship. The luminosity of the image and the use of soft focus lend an atmosphere of mystery and sensuality to the dreamlike scene. The young boy evokes ideal beauty and the horse traditional connotations of virility, manhood, and life transitions.

49. J. CRAIG ANNAN. Scottish, 1864–1946. *Stirling Castle*. 1906. From *Camera Work*, no. 19 (July 1907). Photogravure, 5⅞ × 8½″. Philadelphia Museum of Art: Gift of Carl Zigrosser

James Craig Annan, the second son of photographer Thomas Annan, was born in 1864 near Glasgow. He was a favorite of Alfred Stieglitz, who promoted his work through exhibitions and publication in *Camera Work*. *Stirling Castle* is an example of James Annan's mature style in which he gives a relatively commonplace Scottish scene a sense of foreboding, chiefly through the ghostly illumination of the white horse. Traditionally associated with mystical attributes, the white horse has also symbolized the triumph of goodness over evil.

50. ALFRED STIEGLITZ. American, 1864–1946. *The Street—Design for a Poster*. 1903. Photogravure, 18¾ × 12¾″. Philadelphia Museum of Art: The Alfred Stieglitz Collection

51. ALFRED STIEGLITZ. *Going to the Post*. 1904. Photogravure, 12⅛ × 10⅜″. The Art Institute of Chicago, The Alfred Stieglitz Collection, 1949.841

Stieglitz's innovative photographs and his unrelenting crusade for the medium's recognition as a fine art have made him the pivotal figure in twentieth-century photography. The horse appeared frequently as a subject in Stieglitz's early views of New York after his return from Germany in 1890, as he strove to portray the dynamism of a city in transition. Smaller versions of both *Design for a Poster* and *Going to the Post* were reproduced in *Camera Work*, the celebrated periodical of the Photo-Secessionist movement that was published and edited by Stieglitz from 1903 to 1917. Of the fifty-one Stieglitz photographs in *Camera Work*, twelve show the horse at work.

52. HARRY C. RUBINCAM. American, 1871–1940. *In the Circus*. 1905. From *Camera Work*, no. 17 (January 1907). Photogravure, 6⅛ × 7⅞″. The Minneapolis Institute of Arts, Gift of Julia Marshall

The Englishman Philip Astley, considered the father of the modern circus, developed the riding ring as the basic core around which all the other acts revolved. Trick riding was the central attraction of his first circus in 1768. Another Englishman, John Bill Ricketts, brought the first full-scale circus to the United States. He built an amphitheater in Philadelphia and inaugurated his circus in 1793 in the presence of President George Washington and his wife, Martha. Although Ricketts's circus included a tightrope walker and clowns, its most exciting event was his horse Cornplanter's leaping over the back of another horse. Rubincam's view of a pretty young woman, clad in ballet tutu and standing on the bare back of a galloping horse, is emblematic of the spirit of the circus. Living in Colorado, Rubincam was a distant member of Stieglitz's Photo-Secessionist movement. Little is known of Rubincam's small body of work, and his reputation is built upon this one dynamic image of the circus rider, his only photograph to be illustrated in Stieglitz's publication, *Camera Work*.

53. Photographer unknown. *Eunice Winkless's Dive Into Pool of Water, Pueblo, Colorado, July 4, 1905*. Silver print, 7⅜ × 9½″. Library of Congress, Washington, D.C.

Nothing is known of Eunice Winkless or of the dauntless horse who shared this daredevil dive. Eunice was probably a performer who traveled the county-fair circuit with her spine-tingling act. Quietly experiencing the Fourth of July event with the human spectators is an undoubtedly thankful equine figure coming into the picture frame at the lower left.

54. Photographer unknown. *May Wirth*. c. 1915. Silver print, 3⅝ × 3⅛″. Circus World Museum, Baraboo, Wisconsin

In 1964, May Wirth (1894–1978) became the second living person to receive the greatest honor of the American circus world, induction into the Circus Hall of Fame. Born in Australia, Wirth grew up in the circus and, at the age of three, began learning the basics of tumbling and contortion. Wirth began training for trick bareback riding in 1904 and soon accomplished the somersault, the only woman known to have achieved such a feat. Over the years, she developed her act to include twisted, front, and back somersaults, somersaulting from the back of one horse to that of another, flipping from hands to feet to hands on the back of a galloping horse, jumping from the ground onto the back of a horse, and somersaulting backward through flaming hoops. From 1902 until her retirement in 1934, Wirth toured with the Australian Circuses, the Ringling Bros., Barnum and Bailey, and various vaudeville acts. Part of Wirth's success depended on a certain dapple-gray horse she acquired about 1912. Joe was large, standing 16½ hands, and had a broad back and short legs. He had the perfect build for Wirth's small stature, he was fast, and, most important, his gait was smooth. An unknown photographer has captured here the trust between the great circus performer and her favorite mount, as he gallops steadily around the ring, ever ready to receive his diminutive partner.

55. Photographer unknown. Untitled. 1870s. Albumen print from wet collodion-on-glass negative, 4⅛ × 5⅝″. Courtesy William L. Schaeffer, Chester, Connecticut

In a simple, unpretentious photograph, an anonymous photographer of the nineteenth century illustrates the innate majesty of the horse. The owner or trainer is probably putting this handsome white horse through his paces, perhaps for a performance in a circus or fair. The animal's ability to hold the rearing pose for the exposure time of the photograph is a testament to his concentration, agility, and receptiveness to the discipline imposed by his human master.

56. FRANCES BENJAMIN JOHNSTON. American, 1864–1952. *Agriculture. Animal Life. Studying the Horse*. 1899–1900. From an album of 159 photographs documenting the Hampton Institute, Hampton, Virginia. Platinum print, 7½ × 9½″. The Museum of Modern Art, New York. Gift of Lincoln Kirstein

Johnston was commissioned to photograph the Hampton Institute in 1899–1900 for an exhibition at the Paris Exposition of 1900 that was to illustrate the contemporary life of the American Negro. Established in 1868 during the period of Reconstruction after the Civil War, Hampton trained Black and American Indian youth in domestic and agricultural trades as well as the liberal arts. The institute was integrated and coeducational and emphasized "learning-by-doing." During Johnston's documentation, there were nearly 1,000 students, of whom 135 were American Indians. An early feminist and a niece of Grover Cleveland, Johnston operated a commercial studio in Washington, D.C., that had close ties to the Smithsonian Institution, the Library of Congress, and the White House.

57. FREDERICK W. BREHM. American, 1871–1950. *Police Group Portrait*. c. 1910. Silver print, 9¼ × 22¼″. International Museum of Photography at George Eastman House, Rochester, New York

Brehm joined Eastman Kodak in 1917 and, except for a brief period as a commercial photographer, remained with the company until his death. While at Kodak, he was sent to work at the Mechanics Institute (now the Rochester Institute of Technology) initially as an instructor, but he was ultimately credited with developing its phototech department into one of the most outstanding schools in that burgeoning field. Brehm developed and patented the panoramic "cirkut" camera and, in 1906, created the largest photograph ever made up until that time. The principles involved in the cirkut camera have been used in high-speed photography as well as in strip-exposure aerial cameras. This panorama of the policemen was made with the cirkut camera in the early years of the twentieth century, when the horse was yielding to the technology of the automobile.

58. Photographer unknown. *Horse Portrait: Colorado*. c. 1890. Silver print, 3½″ diameter. Museum of New Mexico, Albuquerque, neg. no. 11142

"You press the button, we do the rest" was the turn-of-the-century slogan that launched a revolution in photography and gave birth to the notion of the snapshot. Frustrated with the unwieldy apparatus of the wet-collodion process, amateur photographer George Eastman resolved to simplify photography and make it available to a larger public. The philosophy of Kodak, Eastman's trademark by 1888, was to separate the work that any ordinary person could do in pushing a button to "take" the photograph from the work in the darkroom that only an expert was equipped to accomplish. Beginning with a dry-plate patent in the early 1880s, Eastman and his partner, William H. Walker, eventually developed a roll-holder for a paper-negative material to be wound by a key after each of twenty-four exposures. Their camera of 1888 contained one hundred exposures, which the customer was to use and send back to the manufacturer for development of prints and reloading of the camera. The negative material gradually improved, and by 1889, Kodak was using transparent celluloid film in its new Number 1 Kodak Camera. This portrait of a horse was made with the larger Number 2 model, which produced a 3½-inch circular negative.

59. HILL AND WATKINS. American, n.d. Untitled. 1890s. Imperial cabinet card, albumen print from wet collodion-on-glass negative, 7½ × 9¼″. Collection Gordon L. Bennett

Human beings often capitalize on their physical peculiarities—the tallest man, the bearded lady, Siamese twins—for the amusement of others at carnivals or circuses. From its earliest days, photography has recorded these oddities. Cartes-de-visite of Tom Thumb and of carnival attractions abound in nineteenth-century photographic albums; there are also numerous representations of the horse with the longest mane and tail. Hill and Watkins's cabinet card memorializes one of these "freak" animals, whose tresses were carefully groomed and whose life was one of passive display. The cabinet card had been introduced in England in 1866. This larger and better-quality format of photographic portraiture presented stiff competition for the carte-de-visite, which had been the rage since its patent by Disdéri in 1854. Cabinet cards were also elaborately imprinted with the photographer's name, and studios continued to vie with one another to photograph celebrities and commercially attractive subjects such as the unusual horse in Hill and Watkins's image.

60. ALFRED STIEGLITZ. *Spiritual America*. 1923. Silver print, 4½ × 3½″. Philadelphia Museum of Art: The Alfred Stieglitz Collection

Throughout his career, Stieglitz was interested in creating diary-like series of photographs. Among his best known are the views of New York City from his various windows, a "composite portrait" of Georgia O'Keeffe, and the cloud sequences he called Equivalents. According to one of his biographers, Dorothy Norman, Stieglitz also contemplated a series of horse photographs on the subject of geldings and stallions. Norman quotes Stieglitz: "In Paris I once saw two teams of black stallions pulling wagons, going along side by side. The traffic was stopped. The horses were lined up in front of me. Along the curb were many women at market. The horses stood there, throbbing, pulsating, their penises swaying half-erect—swaying—shining. I stood there transfixed, regretting that I had no camera with me. No one wished to be seen looking at the animals, yet one could feel that everyone was aware of them, wanting to look. In New York such a thing would not be permitted. All the horses in the city are geldings." In 1923, Stieglitz made this photograph of a gelding and gave it the title *Spiritual America*.

61. CLARENCE KENNEDY. American, 1892–1972. *Legend Hoof of a Bronze Horse Found at the Same Time as the Charioteer at Delphi*. 1928. From part I of volume I of the portfolio series Studies in the History and Criticism of Sculpture. Toned silver print, 10¼ × 6½″. The Art Institute of Chicago. Photography Purchase Fund, 1964.308

After earning a degree in architecture, Kennedy studied the restoration and photography of sculpture in 1920–21. Three years before, he had begun an association with Smith College that lasted until his retirement in 1960 as chairman of the art department and leader of the Smith College seminar in Florence. Although his photographic legacy encompasses technological work on the stereoscopic camera and projection in collaboration with Edwin Land and on the collotype and offset printing with the Meriden Gravure Company, Kennedy is best remembered for his sensitive studies of sculpture and other works of art. His photographic detail of a horse's hoof transcends straight documentation of historical sculpture to attain a simple elegance. The photograph itself becomes a work of art, evoking the abstraction and purity of a Barnett Newman painting.

62. HEIN GORNY. German, 1904–1967. *The Jump*. c. 1930. Silver print, 9 × 6½". Courtesy Sander Gallery, New York

An early student of modern art, Gorny began a career in photography in the mid-1920s. His commercial work was influenced by Albert Renger-Patzsch in its use of patterns and repetitions of shapes to promote the sales of products. Gorny also photographed extensively in rural settings, creating landscapes and animal studies such as this dynamic, modernist image.

63. ALBERT RENGER-PATZSCH. German, 1897–1966. *Pferd am Priel*. c. 1926. Silver print, 9 × 6⅜". Gilman Paper Company Collection

Renger-Patzsch was one of the most influential photographers of the Weimar Republic in Germany (1918–32). He promoted photography for its realism and became a leader of the New Objectivity movement in the 1920s, along with the painters Otto Dix and George Grosz. Renger-Patzsch felt that photography should depict the beauty in objects and their structure, whether in nature or industry. His early work culminated in 1928 with the publication of *Die Welt ist schön*, in which this photograph is illustrated. It is an image that celebrates patterns in nature.

64. HENRI CARTIER-BRESSON. French, born 1908. *Martiques, France*. 1932–33. Silver print, 8⅞ × 5⅞". Courtesy Henri Cartier-Bresson/Magnum Photos, Inc.

Cartier-Bresson, who began his career as a student of Cubist painting, ultimately abandoned photography to return to drawing. However, in the intervening forty years, he devoted himself to seizing what he called "the decisive moment" in photographing the idiosyncrasies of French society. The image of the statue in the southern French town of Martigues is filled with aesthetic and political significance for the photographer. Aided by a Leica camera acquired in 1932 and armed with his own intuitive sense of the moment, Cartier-Bresson has created a visual pun and a truly Surrealist image from an ordinary scene in everyday life. It has been suggested that the assemblage of posters and the compressed, overlapping planes in the background reflect Cartier-Bresson's fascination with the art of the Surrealist collage as well as his early investigation of Cubism. The statue of the boy is part of a monument to the first governor-general of French Indochina. Cartier-Bresson's use of the horse to portray the figure's precarious virility has been said to reflect his feelings about French colonial policies.

65. MANUEL ALVAREZ BRAVO. Mexican, born 1902. *Los Obstáculos*. 1929. Platinum print, 7 × 9¼". Courtesy The Witkin Gallery, Inc., New York

Bravo began his photographic career in Mexico City in 1924. His introduction to Tina Modotti in 1927 brought him in contact with Edward Weston, Diego Rivera, and the mainstream of the great Mexican artists and mural painters. His work incorporates elements of Surrealism with subjects from Mexican life and folklore. The art of carousel carving was flourishing in Mexico in the 1920s when Bravo made this image. Mexican carvers were influenced by the American carousels they had seen in traveling fairs and festivals at the turn of the century. The industry was pioneered by the master artisan Mucio Juarez, a carver of European-style furniture. Mexican carousel horses are often smaller than their American counterparts and have wooden eyes and tails, prominent teeth, bulging muscles, and oversized saddles. Painted or sculpted horses appear in many of Bravo's photographs. This image of carousel horses, straining to free themselves from their tarpaulin cover, is one of his most dynamic and surreal—as if in a dream, inanimate objects are coming to life.

66. ILSE BING. American, born Germany 1899. *Shop Sign, Paris*. 1933. Silver print, 7¾ × 11⅛". Private collection, New York. Courtesy Jill Quasha, New York

A pioneering member of the German New Photography movement, which viewed the world from dramatic angles and vantage points, Bing moved to Paris in 1930 and over the next decade produced some of her most important work. Free-lancing and exhibiting until the onset of World War II, she was interned with her husband as an enemy alien in 1940; both immigrated to the United States in 1941. According to Bing, her time in Paris was spent exploring the streets, always with a Leica in her pocket, photographing what struck her at the moment. This tightly cropped image of the butcher-shop facade, with its strong diagonal composition and upturned camera angle, is an example of Bing's spontaneous method and intuitive sense of abstraction. The surreal effect of the "decapitated" horses' heads and the darkness of the image suggest the approaching horrors of war.

67. GOTTHARD SCHUH. Swiss, 1898–1969. *Cavalry*. c. 1938. Silver print, 3½ × 11½". Gilman Paper Company Collection

In the course of history, whole empires were founded on horseback. The exploits of Alexander the Great, Constantine's victory over Maximus in A.D. 312 for control of the Holy Roman Empire, the Crusades and wars between Moor and Christian, Ghengis Khan's conquest of central Asia, and Osman's founding of the Ottoman Empire were all accomplished through brilliant management of cavalry. Schuh's image is a poetic tribute made in the last days of the mounted soldier.

68. ROBERT CAPA. American, born Hungary, 1913–1954. *Soldiers of the International Brigade, Spain*. 1936. Silver print, 7⅞ × 9⅜". Courtesy Estate of Robert Capa/Magnum Photos, Inc.

At the age of twenty-two, Capa left the "movable feast" atmosphere of Paris in the 1930s and, with Leica in hand, traveled to Spain to record the conflict and devastation of the Civil War there. It was the beginning of a career in which he would capture on film five wars over a period of eighteen years. In his book *Death in the Making* (1938), Capa described this photograph of the cavalry: "The heroic confusion of the first days of the siege gives way to a new sense of order. Cavalry appears! Mounted on sorry nags, a mere sergeant in command, they are nevertheless a nucleus for a new fighting army that is to give good account of itself." The Spanish Civil War was one of the last wars in which the horse would appear on active rather than ceremonial duty. In 1947, together with David Seymour ("Chim") and Henri Cartier-Bresson, Capa founded the cooperative agency Magnum Photos. Seven years later, he was killed by a land mine while covering the war in Indochina.

69. ANDRÉ KERTÉSZ. American, born Hungary, 1894–1985. *Paris*. 1927. Six silver prints, each 4½ × 6⅛". International Museum of Photography at George Eastman House, Rochester, New York

Abandoning a business career in Budapest, Kertész moved to Paris in 1925 to achieve his dream of being a full-time photographer. He became successful as a free-lancer, contributing to the important English, French, and German magazines of the period, and was accepted readily into the Montparnasse circle of avant-garde artists and writers. Kertész's work in Paris was subjectively photojournalistic, characterized by a special lyricism, poignance, and spontaneity. His sequence of photographs depicting a collapsed workhorse, captured quickly with his hand-held camera from a window above, is a tender narrative expressed cinematically.

70. CAS OORTHUYS. Dutch, 1908–1975. Untitled (Taxidermist's Horse). c. 1944. Silver print, 7⅞ × 6⅝". Courtesy Charles Isaacs, Malvern, Pennsylvania

Inspired by De Stijl and Bauhaus artists and by Dutch photographers Paul Schuitema and Piet Zwart, Oorthuys began photographing in the late 1920s. He was an ardent socialist and antifascist, and politics influenced his photography throughout most of his career. As a photojournalist, Oorthuys was a staff photographer for *Wij* and later for the publishing house Contact. During Germany's occupation of the Netherlands, beginning in 1940, he participated in the underground activities of the Dutch resistance. In the same year that he was arrested by the Nazis, he photographed this haunting stuffed taxidermist's horse, standing in the rubble of a bombed-out building. The image, a portrait of isolation and suffering, suggests the plight of the Dutch during the war. Oorthuys subsequently escaped and joined Hidden Camera, a secret organization devoted to recording in photographs Nazi atrocities and Dutch resistance.

71. PAUL STRAND. American, 1890–1976. *White Horse, Ranchos de Taos, New Mexico*. 1932. Silver print, 9⅛ × 11½". Courtesy Aperture Foundation, Inc., Paul Strand Archive

Strand began his studies in photography with Lewis Hine and developed his art through the encouragement of Alfred Stieglitz. He made numerous visits to Stieglitz's gallery, "291," where he came to know the art of Picasso and Braque and where he became sensitized to the notion of photography as an expressive art form. After early successful experimentation with abstraction, Strand returned to the application of photography and film-making to social documentation. As a professional film cameraman, he traveled throughout New England, Canada, the Southwest, and Mexico during the 1920s and 1930s. At the same time, he made still photographs that he called "photographic portraits" of the regions in his travels. Strand's striking image of the white horse evokes the light, atmosphere, and open space of the Southwest.

72. MARTIN MUNKÁCSI. Hungarian, 1896–1963. *Cody, Wyoming, Teton Range*. 1938. Silver print, 10⅝ × 13½". Courtesy Estate of Martin Munkácsi

When the Nazis rose to power in 1934, Munkácsi left Berlin, where he had photographed for the *Berliner Illustrirte Zeitung* and came to the United States. Carmel Snow, editor of *Harper's Bazaar*, was aware of his dynamic sports and fashion photographs and hired him for her innovative fashion magazine. Munkácsi radically altered the studio-based tradition of fashion photography by bringing the models outdoors and encouraging the emotions, activities, and drama that one would experience in real life while wearing such clothes. During his career in fashion photography, Munkácsi never abandoned photojournalism, and it is in connection with his photo-essay *Tranquil West* that he made this rich image capturing the texture and landscape of Western life.

73. THURMAN ROTAN. American, 1903–1991. *San Antonio*. 1932. Silver print, 5¼ × 4⅞". Courtesy Keith de Lellis Fine Arts, New York

Rotan was born in Waco, Texas, and moved to New York City in 1926. A self-taught photographer, he was active in the Pictorial Photographers of America, a group led by Gertrude Käsebier and Clarence White. His style gradually grew more modernist, and he eventually aligned himself with the photographers of the West Coast Group f.64. Imogen Cunningham was especially supportive of his work. In 1932, Rotan exhibited at the Julien Levy Gallery, the citadel of modernist art and photography in New York. Known for his architectural and city views, Rotan became fascinated with the skyscrapers that were dramatically altering the New York skyline in the 1930s. He photographed for many architects and designers, often enhancing his visions of soaring architecture by using a photo-mural format and photomontage. *San Antonio* sharply contrasts the new order of modern technology with the old order symbolized by the horse.

74. MARTINE FRANCK. Belgian, born 1938. *Newcastle on Tyne, England*. 1978. Silver print, 5¾ × 8½". Courtesy Martine Franck/Magnum Photos, Inc.

In 1963, Franck began working as a photographer in the Far East. She subsequently worked in the Time-Life labs in Paris and as an assistant to photographers Eliot Elisofon and Gjon Mili. In 1972, Franck co-founded Viva, a photography collective dedicated to the type of progressive social documentation that more traditional picture agencies and publications found too controversial. As in *Newcastle on Tyne*, where a horse rolls in a field of wild flowers against an industrial background on the horizon, Franck frequently editorializes about the dehumanizing effects of middle-class values by juxtaposing symbols of contradictory attitudes in her photographs. She became a member of Magnum in 1983.

75. BERENICE ABBOTT. American, born 1898. *The El at Columbus Avenue and Broadway*. 1929. Silver print, 6⅜ × 8¾". International Museum of Photography at George Eastman House, Rochester, New York

After nearly a decade in Paris photographing the artists and writers of cafe society, Abbott returned to New York in 1929. The angled and asymmetrical composition of *The El at Columbus Avenue and Broadway* reflects the modernist influences of Abbott's European years, including those photographers who would have shown with her in 1929 at the avant-garde *Film und Foto* exhibition in Stuttgart. One of her last images using the hand-held camera, Abbott's snapshot captures the dynamism of the bustling city as it pivots around the statue of a prancing horse.

76. ROBERT DOISNEAU. French, born 1912. *Les Embarras des Petits Champs*. 1969. Silver print, 7¼ × 9¼″. Courtesy Robert Doisneau/Rapho

Although trained in painting and engraving, Doisneau found his true genius in observing the human condition with a camera. In the 1930s, he earned his living as a commercial photographer and as an industrial photographer in a Renault car factory. During World War II, he was active in the French Resistance, reviving his engraving expertise to make forged passports and identification papers. The sensitive photo reportage for which Doisneau is known today evolved from his photography of the Occupation and Liberation. Roaming the streets of Paris with his camera, he appreciates human foibles and odd moments, like this chance encounter of Paris traffic with a frolicking equestrian monument rising above the fray.

77. ESTHER BUBLEY. American, born 1921. *Rockefeller Center, N.Y.* 1940s. Silver print, 8⅝ × 13″. Private collection, New York

Bubley was initiated into the world of commercial photography through assisting in the laboratory of the Farm Securities Administration, the government agency directed by Roy Stryker and devoted to documenting and publicizing rural poverty during the Great Depression. When Stryker left the FSA to work for Standard Oil of New Jersey (now Exxon), he hired Bubley as one of the photographers to record the worldwide activities of Standard Oil and help improve its public image. Bubley was not yet twenty-five years old when most of these photographs were made. Apart from their propagandistic mission, they form a unique record of the United States after World War II, a time of dramatic social and economic change. Bubley's photograph of the equine hood ornament on an automobile in Rockefeller Center, where Standard Oil's Esso Building was under construction in 1946, evokes the dizzying heights and depths of New York City.

78. WALKER EVANS. American, 1903–1975. *Southeastern U.S.* 1936. Silver print, 8½ × 6½″. The Art Institute of Chicago, Courtesy of Ruttenberg Arts Foundation, 196.1979

In spite of a yearning to write, Evans found his true talent for expression in photography. When he began photographing, in 1929, he was influenced by the extreme compositional devices of European avant-garde photographers, but by the mid-1930s he had developed his own sharp-focus, frontal style with a strong emphasis on subject matter. Although intuitively aesthetic, Evans looked to the documentary examples of Atget and Hine. In his architectural photographs, he was attracted to humble structures with patinas of age. Evans was an inveterate collector of American vernacular objects, from postcards to commercial signs. This fragment of a torn equestrian poster or the facade of the stables in Natchez, Mississippi (plate 81), when captured by Evans in a photograph, became part of his collected experiences.

79. IRVING PENN. American, born 1917. *Pulquería Decoration, Mexico*. 1942. Silver print, 11 × 10¼″. Courtesy Irving Penn

While studying painting at the Philadelphia Museum School of Industrial Art in 1935, Irving Penn met Alexey Brodovitch, who introduced him to the photography of Eugene Atget and Walker Evans. After graduation, Penn worked in New York as a commercial artist and for a brief time as Brodovitch's assistant and eventual successor at Saks Fifth Avenue. In 1941, he went to Mexico to take up his painting again, although *Pulquería Decoration* indicates that he was also experimenting with photography. While the photograph suggests the influence of Evans, it is more significant as an early example of what John Szarkowski has called Penn's "taste for the special beauties of decay and imperfection." This elegant record of Mexican folk art anticipates, in its abstraction and texture, Penn's later Cigarette photographs and Street Material series in the 1970s.

80. EDWARD WESTON. American, 1886–1958. *Salinas, Horses for Sale*. 1939. Silver print, 7½ × 9½″. Center for Creative Photography, Tucson

Folk influences permeated American art between the two world wars: in the work of regionalist painters Grant Wood and Thomas Hart Benton; in the music of Charles Ives, Virgil Thomson, and Aaron Copeland; and in the photography of Charles Sheeler, Walker Evans, and Edward Weston. Objects of Mexican folk art had been the subject of much of Weston's photography from 1923 to 1926, and in 1937–38, his interest in American folk art rekindled during his travels throughout the West on a Guggenheim fellowship. The photographs from these trips, including those of the Salinas horse barn and the K. B. Dude Ranch (plate 83), were published in *California and the West* (1940). Weston, like Evans, was fascinated with rural vernacular architecture and the art in signage. When the sliding doors on the Salinas barn are brought together, a striking circular painting appears of a cowboy cooking over a campfire. The geometry and simplicity of form in the image also must have appealed to Weston's modernist aesthetic.

81. WALKER EVANS. *Stables, Natchez, Mississippi*. March 1935. Silver print, 10 × 8″. Gilman Paper Company Collection

See note for plate 78.

82. WRIGHT MORRIS. American, born 1910. *Bedroom, Home Place*. 1947. Silver print, 8 × 10″. Courtesy Wright Morris

Morris is well known as a novelist, but in the decade between 1938 and 1947, he became intensely involved in the art of photography. Like Walker Evans, Morris was drawn to the simple artifacts and architecture of the American vernacular. With the assistance of two Guggenheim fellowships, he produced *The Inhabitants* (1946) and *The Home Place* (1948), in which this photograph appears. In 1947, Morris returned to his roots in Nebraska and made a series of photographs in Chapman and at the "home place," his Uncle Harry's farm in Norfolk. In an image reminiscent of Evans's photographs of walls in Southern sharecroppers' homes, Morris has created a beautiful vignette of randomly scattered shapes and textures on a modest bedroom wall. Coincidentally, a variant of the naive painting of black-and-white horses, a common rural motif, appears in Evans's photograph of the stable facade in Natchez, Mississippi (plate 81).

83. EDWARD WESTON. *K. B. Dude Ranch*. 1938. Silver print, 7½ × 9½″. Center for Creative Photography, Tucson

In his travels through the West for a Guggenheim project, Weston sought to find the true American aesthetic in naive art and anonymous objects. Pointing the camera sharply upward, he made the sign for the K. B. Dude Ranch innocently evoke the myth of Pegasus soaring over the Western landscape.

84. HAROLD E. EDGERTON. American, 1903–1990. *Rodeo*. 1940. Silver print, 8⅜ × 7″. Courtesy Palm Press, Inc.

During the two decades prior to the American Civil War, the rodeo was evolving as a sport in the Mexican territory of Texas; its language, composed of words like bronco, lasso, and lariat, reflects this Spanish origin. The first recorded rodeo in the United States, with cowboys participating from different ranches, took place in 1869 and featured bronco-busting, calf roping, and riding tricks. The original bronco-busting event, as illustrated in Edgerton's photograph, was intended to showcase a cowboy's ability to subdue an unbroken horse. Today, bronco-busting is manipulated and governed by rules—the horse is provoked by a bucking strap, and the cowboy is required to apply a certain amount of spur. Judging of the event is based on time, style, the spirit of the horse, and the boldness of the rider. Dr. Harold Edgerton, the inventor of stroboscopic photography, has frozen the moment, invisible to the eye, when horse and rider are separated and suspended in space.

85. Photographer unknown. *Triple Dead Heat, Windsor,* 1923. Silver print, 17 × 23⅜″. Gilman Paper Company Collection

In 1665, the first American Thoroughbred racecourse was built on Long Island. The sport did not blossom, however, until a breeder from Virginia purchased the twenty-one-year-old British stallion Diomed, winner of the first Epsom Derby in 1780. Diomed had been unsuccessful at stud in England, but in the United States, he was still siring winning horses at the age of twenty-nine. After the Civil War, racing prospered, and the great races that compose the American Triple Crown were established: the Belmont Stakes in 1867, the Preakness Stakes in 1873, and the Kentucky Derby in 1876. Except for the period between the turn of the century and the 1920s, when severe legislation curbed racing and betting, Thoroughbred racing has been one of the most popular spectator sports in the United States. This unusual triple dead heat occurred in September 1923 between the horses Dinkie, Dumas, and Marvex.

86. EDWARD J. STEICHEN. American, born Luxembourg, 1879–1973. *Gallant Fox and Landry*. 1930. Silver print, 7⅝ × 9⅝″. Gilman Paper Company Collection

Neil Newman (also known as "Roamer"), the respected chronicler of Thoroughbred racing, wrote the following epitaph: "Since the retirement of Man o' War no horse has captured the imagination of the American public as has Gallant Fox. . . . He swept like a meteor across the racing sky in 1930. . . . He was more than a race horse—he was an institution." Born in 1927, the bay colt was the son of Marguerite and Sir Gallahad III. Steichen photographed Gallant Fox with his regular jockey, Earl Sande, the year they teamed up to make the colt the second American horse to win the Triple Crown. "The Fox" also became the first Thoroughbred to win over three hundred thousand dollars in a single year. At the end of 1930, owner William Woodward retired his prize horse to stud. With the notable exceptions of siring the next Triple Crown winner, Omaha, and two Ascot Gold Cup champions, Flares and Granville, Gallant Fox's stud career was less dramatic than his performance at the track. He died in 1954 an hour before the running of the Gallant Fox Handicap in Jamaica, New York, and the Marguerite Stakes at Pimlico.

87. ALEXANDER MIKHAILOVICH RODCHENKO. Russian, 1891–1956. *Jockeys*. 1935. Silver print, 4 × 6″. Courtesy Robert Koch Gallery, San Francisco

For a twenty-year period beginning about 1921, Rodchenko abandoned painting and dedicated himself to the arts of photography and photomontage, exploring their formal as well as political possibilities. He became the chief representative in Russia of the New Photography movement, born in Germany in the 1920s. Based on the concept of a shifting world, the movement encouraged the use of close-up, dramatic, and distorting angles as well as high and low viewpoints of familiar objects and sights. Together with his friend El Lissitzky, Rodchenko photographed and designed covers for books, Russian Constructivist publications, and political magazines of the new Socialist society. Ultimately, he was criticized in his own country for imitating foreign photography and emphasizing form over content. Using the snapshot as his principal format, Rodchenko brought to images such as *Jockeys* the sensation of speed, power, and intensity that characterized a period of turbulence.

88. BOWDEN BROTHERS, LONDON. English studio, dates unknown. *Polo Tournament, London: White's Club vs. Bath Club*. c. 1900. Collodio-chloride print, 4¼ × 5⅞″. Gernsheim Collection, Harry Ransom Humanities Research Center, University of Texas at Austin

Polo dates back to the 4th century B.C., when the cavalry of Darius played a similar game before Alexander the Great conquered the Persian Empire. For more than two thousand years, the game was confined to the Near and Far East; it derives its name from the Tibetan word for ball (*pulu*). In the mid-nineteenth century, the British discovered polo in India and became enthusiastic players, soon sending the sport home for the amusement of the aristocracy. A few decades later, with the introduction of the hand-held camera, faster lenses, and more sensitive films, the Bowden Brothers of London were able to record a moment of arrested action in this sport.

89. MAN RAY. American, 1890–1976. *Polo Player*. c. 1935. Silver print, 6⅜ × 8¾″. Collection Alice Adam, Chicago

Man Ray's lifelong career as a painter was punctuated by intense periods of photographic experimentation beginning around 1918. Although he had previously used photography to document his paintings, he gradually became sensitive to its power as an art form itself—largely through visits to the pioneering exhibitions of photography and modern art at Stieglitz's gallery, "291." At this time, he also met the artist Marcel Duchamp, who introduced him to the New York Dada movement. Man Ray's early photographic efforts were associated with Dada: he photographed ready-made objects and assembled ready-mades that were subsequently destroyed, their existence validated solely by a photographic print. In 1921, Man Ray followed Duchamp to Paris, where he became involved with the European Dadaists and Surrealists. This dreamlike vision of a polo-player marionette galloping across a display window combines Man Ray's preoccupation with the found object and his acute sense of the surreal context.

90. PAUL OUTERBRIDGE, JR. American, 1896–1959. *Equestrian Still Life*. 1924. Platinum print, 4⅝ × 6". Courtesy Estate of Paul Outerbridge, Jr.

In 1924, Outerbridge was a successful commercial photographer who published his work in *Vanity Fair* and *Harper's Bazaar*. He had studied at the Clarence White School of Photography, where his distinguished classmates included Margaret Bourke-White, Ralph Steiner, Doris Ullman, and Laura Gilpin. Outerbridge became known for his small, exquisite still lifes, printed in platinum and evocative of affluent living. In this equestrian tableau, a nineteenth-century print entitled *The Duchess* acts as a background for the aristocratic trappings of a hunt or a formal ride in the country.

91. BERENICE ABBOTT. *Harness Shop Horse*. 1930. Silver print, 9½ × 7½". Gilman Paper Company Collection

Soon after her return to New York from Paris in 1929, Abbott began a photographic documentation of the city, much as Atget had done in Paris and its environs at the turn of the century and into the 1920s. Initially, Abbott supported her project by taking on free-lance assignments. In 1935, however, she won financial assistance from the Federal Art Project of the Works Progress Administration; with that help, she continued her documentation until its culmination in 1939 with the publication of her first book, *Changing New York*. The New York photographs, of which *Harness Shop Horse* is an early example, were made with an 8 × 10 view camera. The handsome carving of the horse outside the shop served as an advertisement for the equestrian wares inside, but its utilitarian purpose would eventually yield to its value as an example of folk art from a vanishing era.

92. AGNÈS BONNOT. French, born 1949. *Hippodrome de Vincennes*. 1984. Silver print, 7 × 6⅝". Courtesy Agnès Bonnot/Agence VU

Bonnot is a commercial photographer, working on assignment for fashion, advertising, and editorial clients, particularly in the performing arts. She won the coveted Prix Niépce in 1987 and recently has been absorbed in a commission to photograph the Trisha Brown dance company in Belgium. Bonnot's image of the harness-racing horse, with its theatrical lighting and precarious viewpoint, is part of a series on racing that she photographed for the daily newspaper *Libération* and subsequently assembled into a book, *Chevaux Photographies*.

93. A. AUBREY BODINE. American, 1906–1970. *Maryland Hunt Cup*. c. 1950. Toned silver print, 13½ × 11". Courtesy Kathleen Ewing Gallery, Washington, D.C.

Bodine has portrayed a disheartening moment in what is perhaps the most demanding of the horse sports, the steeplechase. Usually Thoroughbreds are chosen for this event who have the ability to run at a high speed over a course nearly five miles long, with as many as thirty major obstacles to negotiate. Although they may start their career on the flat, steeplechasers are prized more for their jumping skill and stamina than their speed. When flat racers are retired to stud or brood at five or six years, many steeplechasers are just embarking on their career. Males are considered faster and stronger than mares and fillies; geldings are preferred for their calmer temperaments and ability to retain weight, which gives them more staying power in longer races. In his work for the Baltimore *Sunday Sun* from 1927 until his death in 1970, Bodine was an award-winning photojournalist. At the same time, combining the style of rigorous newspaper photography with a painterly pictorialist aesthetic, he earned an international reputation in salon exhibitions.

94. MARIAN POST WOLCOTT. American, 1910–1990. *Sulky Race, Mercer County, Kentucky*. 1940. Silver print, 7 × 9⅜". Library of Congress, Washington, D.C.

The first horse-drawn conveyance was probably the two-wheeled cart, or chariot. Originally used in hunting and war, the chariot became a racing vehicle with the Greeks and Romans. In modern harness racing, the bicycle-wheeled sulky was introduced in 1895 to replace an earlier high-wheeled version, and by 1897 a horse could cover a mile in less than two minutes. The Standardbred is the principal trotting and pacing breed in the United States, Europe, and Australia; the Hambletonian fleet trotters are the most celebrated of the nineteenth- and early-twentieth-century bloodlines. The prestigious Grand Circuit, established for racing trotters in the nineteenth century, culminates in the Hambletonian in Illinois. Formerly a feature of county and state fairs, the racing of trotters and faster pacers has become an international business, with nearly a thousand racetracks in the United States alone. Two years before Wolcott made this photograph for the Standard Oil Project, Billy Direct ran a mile in one minute fifty-five seconds, breaking by a quarter second the 1906 record of the greatest harness pacer of all time, Dan Patch.

95. BRASSAÏ (Gyula Halász). French, born Transylvania, 1899–1984. *The Royal Show, England*. 1959. Silver print, 11⅜ × 9¼". Collection Gérard Lévy and François LePage, Paris

Dubbed "the eye of Paris" in the 1930s by Henry Miller, Brassaï was obsessed with recording the bohemian characters of the Parisian art world by day and the seamy underworld denizens of its streets, clubs, and brothels by night. Over the years, he exhibited and published several books of photographs and free-lanced for photo agencies, his eye ever alert to disparate life-styles. With a characteristic sense of humor, he has focused his lens here on an atypical subject and captured the serious mood of preparation for a dressage test at the Royal Show in England. The term *dressage* derives from the French word for training and finds its origins in the medieval courts of Europe. Comparable to school figures in Olympic figure-skating competitions, dressage measures the agility and precision of the horse, the subtle control of the rider, and the harmony of the two working together. Depending upon the class level, the dressage test lasts from 7.5 to 15 minutes and is carefully orchestrated to include various gaits and complex movements and figures in a standard-size arena.

96. LEONARD FREED. American, born 1929. *Sale of the Yearlings in Deauville, France*. 1964. Silver print, 10¼ × 14⅞". Courtesy Leonard Freed/Magnum Photos, Inc.

By definition of the first *British General Stud Book* (1791), all Thoroughbreds are descended from three stallions imported into Great Britain during the late seventeenth and early eighteenth centuries: the Byerly Turk (1686), the Godolphin Barb (1730), and the Darley Arabian (1704). The evolution of the Thoroughbred reflects the first systematic development of a breed; it is also the oldest breed for which meticulous records exist. Since the breed is now closed, the sire and dam of any foal must be registered in one of the acceptable stud books. As a photographer, Freed is an acute observer of life-styles as diverse as the artistocratic Thoroughbred auction in France shown here and the civil-rights struggle of American Blacks in the sixties. Using his camera in the service of a social conscience, he is well known for his objectivity and for his association with other "concerned photographers" in the tradition of Hine and Riis.

97. EDWARD J. STEICHEN. *White*. 1935. Silver print, 7½ × 9½". International Museum of Photography at George Eastman House, Rochester, New York

The use of live animals in fashion photography gained prominence in the 1930s, about the same time that photographers like Munkácsi were beginning to abandon passive studio shots of "the model as still life" for outdoor action shots. Initially, the use of horses in fashion photographs was associated with sporting or country attire. In response to an earlier photograph entitled *Black*, an image of a black grand piano with models in black dresses, Steichen, perhaps jokingly, created *White* for the January 1936 issue of *Vogue*. For the occasion of this fashion photograph, Steichen brought a pure white horse into the studio to accompany three white-clad models posed friezelike against white tile, reminiscent to some of a lavatory. Considered static and retrograde by most critics, the photograph met with a controversial reception that ironically has made it one of Steichen's more familiar fashion works.

98. ANSEL ADAMS. American, 1902–1984. *Saddle*. 1929. Silver print, 6 × 8". Collection Gordon L. Bennett

Adams made this previously unpublished photograph of a saddle three years before he joined forces with Edward Weston, Imogen Cunningham, and Willard Van Dyck to form Group f.64, dedicated to the promotion of straight, unmanipulated photography. According to his widow, Virginia Adams, the saddle belonged to Donald Tressider, president of Yosemite Park and Curry Company and later president of Stanford University. The photograph was made in connection with a commission from Tressider in the late 1920s and the 1930s to record certain aspects of Yosemite for promotional purposes. The print is probably unique, since a fire in 1937 destroyed most of Adams's negatives from this period. This image evokes the purity and stark elegance of Adams's earlier masterpiece *Monolith, the Face of Half Dome* (1927).

99. PAUL STRAND. *Harness, Luzzara, Italy*. 1953. Silver print, 9⅝ × 7⅝". Courtesy Aperture Foundation, Inc., Paul Strand Archive

In 1952, while searching for a European village in which to set down roots, Strand began collaborating on a book about an Italian village with the screenwriter Cesare Zavattini. They chose as their subject Zavattini's hometown of Luzzara, and Strand and his wife spent two months there while the photographer chronicled the town and its people. *Un Paese*, with Italian text by Zavattini, was published in Europe in 1955. This richly textured photograph of a harness is part of the Luzzara essay. Its dense, tapestry-like effect contrasts sharply with the austere beauty of Adams's saddle (plate 98).

100. BILL BRANDT. English, born Germany, 1904–1983. *The White Horse Near Westbury*. c. 1946. Silver print, 8¾ × 7½". Collection Alexandra R. Marshall

The county of Wiltshire is home to most of the hillside horse carvings in England. The Westbury White Horse was made in 1778, supposedly on the site of an earlier horse commemorating the spot where King Alfred won a decisive victory against the Danes. Measuring 166 feet long and 163 feet high, the horse was restored in 1873; in 1957, it was recut and lined with cement. Following World War II, England's most celebrated twentieth-century photographer, Bill Brandt, turned away from his earlier style of straight photo-documentation toward a more poetic, brooding imagery, creating landscapes that were both atmospheric and seemingly uninhabited. The Westbury Horse is part of a series of photographs of the British landscape Brandt made between 1945 and 1950, culminating in the publication in 1951 of *Literary Britain*.

101. WALTER ROSENBLUM. American, born 1919. *Horse, Gaspé, Canada*. 1949. Silver print, 10½ × 13½". Courtesy Walter Rosenblum/fotomann, inc., New York

In 1937, Rosenblum joined the Photo League, a group committed to using photography as an agent of social change through objective documentation of the human condition. Serving several terms as its president and as editor of its publication, *Photo Notes*, Rosenblum was a dedicated participant in the league, whose membership also included Paul Strand and Aaron Siskind. He served in World War II as both a still photographer and a film cameraman for the U.S. Army Signal Corps, seeing combat that included the D-Day landing in Normandy; he was the most decorated American photographer in the war. Shortly after his return, Rosenblum made this quiet image of an old horse resting in a pasture in Gaspé. Unusual in its intimacy and eye-level viewpoint, the image suggests the same quality of compassion that Rosenblum brings to his images of humanity.

102. PAUL STRAND. *Tir a'Mhurain, South Uist, Hebrides*. 1954. Silver print, 9⅜ × 11⅜". Courtesy Aperture Foundation, Inc., Paul Strand Archive

In 1950, after the publication of his book *Time in New England*, Strand and his future wife moved to France, partly because of the repressive political climate in the United States. They traveled extensively in search of the perfect village in which they could live and Strand could photograph, eventually settling in Orgeval, France, in 1955. On a trip to the Hebrides in 1954, Strand made this photograph of horses grazing in a unique pasture at sea on the island of South Uist (Outer Hebrides). It was published in his book *Tir a'Mhurain, Outer Hebrides* (1962).

103. ROBERT FRANK. American, born Switzerland 1924. *Valencia, Spain.* 1951–52. Silver print, 9¼ × 13¾". Courtesy Robert Frank/Pace MacGill Gallery, New York

Arriving in New York in 1947, Frank found employment as a fashion photographer at *Harper's Bazaar* under its art director, Alexey Brodovitch. From 1950 to 1952, he traveled and photographed throughout Peru, France, Spain, and England. In this critical period of his work, Frank gradually abandoned the influence of Kertész and Cartier-Bresson and developed his own style of bittersweet commentary that would culminate in the publication of his controversial book *The Americans* (1959). In *Valencia, Spain,* the silent void in the center and the lurking tensions at the edges of the image, in the guise of a toy horse and galloping horse and rider, express an uneasiness that would pervade his portrait of 1950s America.

104. DOROTHEA LANGE. American, 1895–1965. *Terrified Horse, Berryessa Valley, California.* 1956. Silver print, 6⅝ × 9⅝". The Oakland Museum, California

After studies with photographers Arnold Genthe and Clarence White, Lange left the East Coast in 1918 and opened a portrait gallery in San Francisco. The stock market crash of 1929 prompted her to abandon her artistic portraits of wealthy Bay Area families and turn her camera to the street and its scenes of labor unrest, unemployment, and homelessness. From 1935 to 1939, Lange worked for the Farm Securities Administration, a government agency established to publicize and aid the plight of the poor and unemployed. Traveling throughout twenty-two states, she recorded the lives of migrant workers, sharecroppers, and tenant farmers. Lange was convinced that her photographs, like those of Lewis Hine a few years before, would bring help to her subjects. Her mission to photograph the disenfranchised continued after the Depression, and in 1956, she photographed *Terrified Horse* in connection with a photo essay entitled "Death of a Valley" (in collaboration with photographer Pirkle Jones). Forty-five miles north of San Francisco, a small, fertile valley community was undergoing complete eradication. Farmers and cattlemen were being relocated, and the town of Monticello was being leveled in order to flood the valley and make a reservoir for rapidly growing towns and cities nearby. Lange's image of a horse running scared in the desolate, recently bulldozed landscape is an early example of ecologically concerned photography.

105. ELLIOTT ERWITT. American, born France 1928. *Brazil.* 1970. Silver print, 8 × 12". Courtesy Elliot Erwitt/Magnum Photos, Inc.

An early student of photojournalism, Erwitt joined Magnum Photos following army service in World War II. His photographs are characterized by their sense of humor and their intuitive grasp of poignant situations involving human beings, animals, and the worlds in which they interact. Here, Erwitt has frozen a moment when three men are confounded by a broken-down truck, while the outmoded horse, the only reliable means of transport in sight, stands idle.

106. DENNIS STOCK. American, born 1928. *The Alamo.* 1959. Silver print, 13¼ × 10½". Courtesy Dennis Stock/Magnum Photos, Inc.

Photographer and film maker Dennis Stock worked as an apprentice to the photographer Gjon Mili from 1947 to 1951. In 1951, he distinguished himself by winning the first prize in *Life* magazine's Young Photographers Contest, and he also began his long association with Magnum. Stock, who has published numerous books on his travels and experiences, has had his own film-production company, Visual Objectives, Inc., since 1968. In the mid-1950s, he was working in Hollywood photographing James Dean, a project that would culminate in the publication of two books of photographs on the young actor. Stock later made this almost surreal image of horse props while photographing the filming of the movie *The Alamo.*

107. HENRI CARTIER-BRESSON. *Stud Farm, Touques (Calvados).* 1968. Silver print, 6⅝ × 9⅞". Courtesy Henri Cartier-Bresson/Magnum Photos, Inc.

A mare usually comes into "season" at regular intervals of between eighteen and twenty-one days, at which time she may be bred with a stallion. Today, stallions usually remain at their home stud farm, and mares are brought to them for breeding throughout the spring and early summer. A horse called a "teaser" is used initially to insure that the mare is ready to accept the stallion. The stallion is introduced to mount or "cover" the mare, and the actual mating procedure lasts one to two minutes. If the insemination is successful, the mare will carry the foal for about eleven months. Cartier-Bresson's documentary photograph departs from the realm of art to graphically depict a typical scene: the mare is held very still during the process, prevented from kicking by hobbling her back legs, and further controlled with a twitch in her mouth.

108. EVE ARNOLD. American, born 1913. *The Misfits.* 1961. Silver print, 9⅞ × 6⅝". Courtesy Eve Arnold/Magnum Photos, Inc.

Born in Philadelphia to Russian immigrant parents, Arnold began photographing in 1946. After studying with Brodovitch in 1948, she became associated with Magnum in 1951 and achieved full membership in 1957. Arnold has traveled the world, photographing on assignment for all the major magazines as well as gathering images for her many books. Her photograph of Clark Gable and the wild horse from the film *The Misfits* reveals the spirit and explosive energy of the horse—a quality that human beings have often been tempted to tame and control.

109. DAVID HURN. English, born 1934. *The Last of the Mustang Round-ups, Arizona.* 1980. Silver print, 6¼ × 9⅜". Courtesy David Hurn/Magnum Photos, Inc.

Photographer and teacher David Hurn became interested in photography during his course of study at the Royal Military Academy from 1952 to 1954. After various apprenticeships, he worked as a freelancer in London; his first major assignment was to cover the Hungarian Revolution. In 1973, he became head of the school of film and photography at Gwent College of Higher Education in Newport, Wales. During his tenure in 1979–80 as Distinguished Visiting Artist and Adjunct Professor at Arizona State University in Tempe, Hurn made this photograph of cowboys capturing and subduing a wild mustang. The helpless animal—descendant of the horse ridden by the sixteenth-century conquistadors—looks surprisingly human in its diminished scale and anthropomorphic stance. There is an irony to this familiar Western scene in which the already domesticated horses participate in the enslavement of one of their own.

110. RENÉ BURRI. Swiss, born 1933. *Gaucho, Argentina.* 1958. Silver print, 11⅝ × 7⅝". Courtesy René Burri/Magnum Photos, Inc.

From the early eighteenth century until the influx of European farmers in the late nineteenth century, the South American cowboy, or gaucho, was a familiar figure on the grassy plains of the Argentine pampa. Although agricultural products have since dominated the area, livestock has remained a major industry in Argentina, and photographer René Burri has dramatically captured a living symbol of this continued existence. Known for their agility in cattle roping, gauchos use bolas, sets of two or three heavy balls attached to leather thongs. One of the most recognized photojournalists of his generation, Burri has worked extensively for *Life* magazine and is a member of Magnum.

111. LUCIEN CLERGUE. French, born 1934. *La Pique, Nîmes.* 1964. Silver print, 11¾ × 8¼". Courtesy Lucien Clergue

In the contest between man and bull, no one is as defenseless as the horse, who is a helpless victim rather than a true participant. At an early point in the carefully scripted bullfight, the picador is called upon to ride his horse, usually an old one, close enough to the bull to provoke him into a rage, making him a worthy opponent for the torero, or bullfighter. The horse wears blinkers or a blindfold over one eye to lessen his fear of the bull and a padded apron in case the bull charges upward. However, in the worst scenario, the bull may lower his horns and penetrate the underbelly of the mount, insuring a prolonged death. A team of donkeys then hauls the dying horse from the ring. The Moors, who brought bullfighting to Spain, did not use the picador; his role was initiated by the Spanish. Clergue's photograph is part of an extensive photo essay on the bullfight in Nîmes. From a particularly striking vantage point, the photographer has managed to capture that crucial moment when the horse's life truly hangs in the balance.

112. PETER LAYTIN. American, born 1949. *Carousel No. 1.* 1972. Silver print, 8¾ × 5⅝". Courtesy Peter Laytin

The word *carousel* derives from *carosellos* (little wars), a twelfth-century Arabian game of horsemanship in which perfumed clay balls were tossed from rider to rider, the point being to catch them cleanly and thus avoid the stigma of an unmanly fragrance. In France, these games became *carrousels,* tournaments filled with pageantry and drama. The form of the modern carousel has its roots in late-seventeenth-century French jousting contests involving legless wooden horses mounted on a central pole, initially rotated by man, horse, or mule. Gustav Dentzel, a young German immigrant, pioneered the art of the carousel in America, opening his own company in Philadelphia in 1867. The handcrafted wooden carousel figure, ultimately yielding to cast aluminum and fiberglass, has today entered the realm of the collectible object. Carousel animals often have highly expressive faces and gestures, as does the horse in Laytin's almost horrifying photograph. Laytin, a teacher and critic, has long been associated with the MIT Creative Photography Lab and Gallery.

113. JOSEF KOUDELKA. French, born Czechoslovakia 1938. *Spain.* 1973. Silver print, 5⅞ × 8⅞". Courtesy Josef Koudelka/Magnum Photos, Inc.

114. JOSEF KOUDELKA. *Romania.* 1968. Silver print, 6¼ × 9½". Courtesy Josef Koudelka/Magnum Photos, Inc.

Born in Moravia, Koudelka left his homeland in 1970 to travel throughout Europe, chronicling various festivals and scenes of everyday life. (He remained stateless until 1987, when he became a French citizen.) In Spain, he photographed a mass of corralled wild horses delighting a cheering and picture-snapping crowd. It is an image of displacement, terror, broken spirit, and alienation that must have had special meaning for a man who had only recently chosen a life of exile. Before making that choice, Koudelka had documented another kind of exile living closer to home. His photographs of the Gypsies in Romania were made in 1968, the same year the Warsaw Pact armies invaded Prague. From their first appearance in Western Europe, in the early fourteenth century, nomadic Gypsies have alternately received begrudging acceptance from conventional society and flat rejection as anachronistic troublemakers. Koudelka's photograph was made at a time when a particular government scheme to relocate the Gypsies had recently collapsed. Since that time, little has changed—some Gypsies continue to hold on tenuously to their traditional ways, while others have made attempts to assimilate. Illiteracy and alienation present a bleak future. Koudelka's photograph depicts a happier view, representing the strong bond between Gypsy and horse, the animal at the core of Gypsy life and mythology.

115. ALEN MACWEENEY. American, born Ireland 1939. *White Horse, Donegal.* 1965. Silver print, 8¼ × 8¼". Courtesy Alen MacWeeney

In 1955, at the age of sixteen, the Dublin-born MacWeeney became a photographer for *The Irish Times.* In 1963 he came to New York to apprentice with Richard Avedon. Returning later to Ireland to create a photographic essay evoking the poetry of William Butler Yeats, MacWeeney discovered a tinker camp on the outskirts of Dublin and began a relationship with the tinkers that would allow him to record with camera and tape recorder their life and rituals. Little is known of the Irish tinkers' origins, but it seems likely that they share the same roots as the Romany Gypsies. They, too, are nomads, traveling with horses, caravans, and tents. They live outside conventional society, speaking a secret language, telling fortunes at country fairs, and trading shrewdly in everything from rags and scrap metal to their precious horses. The tinkers have mystical relationships with their animals, and some families claim to have magical horses protecting them. Other tinker tales speak of horses who fly. MacWeeney's monumental images of the horse standing majestically on the crest of an Irish hillside and the glowing white pony at the Clifden Horse Fair (plate 117) suggest there is some truth to the tinkers' superstitions.

116. BRUCE DAVIDSON. American, born 1933. *Welsh Pony.* 1965. Silver print, 6½ × 9⅞". Courtesy Bruce Davidson/Magnum Photos, Inc.

Its diminutive size made the pony ideal for pulling carts of ore from British mine shafts until the end of World War I. But with the onset of modernization, the little horse, standing 14.2 hands or less, was generally limited to circus-performing or other amusements for children. Ponies are cold-bloods in origin and have been subject to frequent mixed breeding, especially with the Arabian bloodline. The greatest variety of pony breeds exists in the British Isles, among them the Welsh Mountain Pony or the more refined Welsh Pony, illustrated in Bruce Davidson's photograph. Davidson was barely a teenager when he began working after school for a professional photographer. After college and military service, he began free-lancing for *Life* magazine and became a member of Magnum in 1959. He has been recognized for his in-depth photo essays on civil-rights activities in the 1960s, Brooklyn teenage gangs, Harlem, and the New York subway. This haunting image of the Welsh pony is part of a series on Welsh miners.

117. ALEN MACWEENEY. *White Pony, Clifden Horse Fair, Ireland*. 1965. Silver print, 8½ × 8½". Courtesy Alen MacWeeney

See note for plate 115.

118. ELIOT PORTER. American, 1901–1990. *Painted Horses on Barn Door, Cundiyo, New Mexico*. 1961. Silver print, 9½ × 7¼". Courtesy Eliot Porter/Scheinbaum & Russek Gallery Ltd, Santa Fe

After graduation from Harvard Medical School in 1929, Porter worked for the next few years in the Radiation Laboratory at MIT and later as an instructor at the medical school. In a dramatic career shift, he became a free-lance photographer in 1944. Porter began his second career as a photographer of birds and eventually expanded his subject matter to include landscapes of particular geological and botanical interest. An ardent conservationist, he traveled the world and created magnificent black-and-white and color photographs, which were ultimately assembled into books and portfolios, many under the auspices of the Sierra Club. He also photographed archaeological and architectural subjects in Greece, Egypt, and Mexico. Porter brings the same scientific reverence for texture and detail to *Barn Door, Cundiyo, New Mexico*, a relic of vernacular architecture, that he displayed in all his studies of nature.

119. GORDON PARKS. American, born 1912. *Lancaster County Barnyard of Christian Cleck (?), Amish Vegetable and Tobacco Farmer Near Coatesville*. April 1946. Silver print, 12½ × 9⅞". Standard Oil of New Jersey Collection, Photographic Archives, University of Louisville

The Amish emigrated to the United States from Central Europe in the early eighteenth century and initially settled in the Lancaster area of Pennsylvania. They sought religious freedom and the possibility of owning their own farmland. The Amish are known for their pacifism, utilitarianism, noncompetitive spirit, and allegiance to God over country. Although today they have had to yield to limited mechanization, the horse is still their main source of power, providing transportation, energy for running farm machinery, and fertilizer for the fields. The Amish live by the following adage: "A horse reproduces, a tractor produces nothing but debts." The photograph made by Gordon Parks for the Standard Oil Project portrays the horse buggy and barn, icons of Amish existence. Although no horses are present, the atmosphere is charged with their presence.

120. O. WINSTON LINK. American, born 1914. *"Maud" Bows to the Virginia Creeper, Green Cove, Virginia*. 1956. Silver print, 16 × 20". Courtesy O. Winston Link/fotomann, inc., New York

From 1955 to 1960, Link made 2,032 negatives of the Norfolk & Western Railway to document the final days of the steam engine before the advent of diesel. Built in the 1850s, the N & W ran from Norfolk, Virginia, on the Atlantic Coast through the Blue Ridge Mountains and the Alleghenies to Columbus, Ohio, and from Hagerstown in the North to Winston-Salem in the South. Link is highly skilled in multiple-flashlight photography, and many of the photographs depict trains in motion at night. Writer Rupert Martin said of Link's imagery, "The richness of this work resides in the simplicity and naïvety of vision and in its evocation of a time past. Link gives us a vernacular portrait of rural American life in the late fifties, whose charm and optimism contrasts with Robert Frank's bleak vision of urban alienation in *The Americans* made at the same time" (p. 3). Link photographed "Maud" on the fifty-five-mile-long Abingdon branch of the N & W in Virginia and North Carolina, near White Top, the highest point of any railroad east of the Rockies. The horse appears to be bowing in deference to the great "iron horse" rounding the curve into the Green Cove station.

121. JEROME LIEBLING. American, born 1924. *Browning, Montana*. 1962. Silver print, 10⅛ × 10¼". Courtesy Jerome Liebling

In the course of his education at Brooklyn College and the New School for Social Research, Liebling studied photography and film with Walter Rosenblum, Paul Strand, and Lewis Jacobs. Since 1970, he has taught at Hampshire College in Massachusetts. In 1960 film maker Jerome Hill commissioned Liebling and Allen Downes to make a film about the Blackfoot Indians of Montana. Hill's grandfather had founded the Great Northern Railroad, and as a child he had often ridden the train from Chicago to Montana. Hill had many fond memories of the Blackfoot Indians, who had worked for the railroad and performed ceremonies and dances in large Eastern cities to attract potential passengers, and he wanted the film to reflect those feelings. However, Liebling and Downes did not see the Blackfoot people in the same nostalgic terms, and their film, *The Old Men* (1963), combined the grandeur and spirituality of the Blackfoot past with the rather bleak present they encountered. While capturing the beauty and poignance of the Blackfoot Indians, the film is bittersweet in its evocation of a lost era, as is this still photograph taken during the filming.

122. DANNY LYON. American, born 1942. *The Boss, Texas*. 1968. Silver print, 5¾ × 8½". Courtesy Danny Lyon/Magnum Photos, Inc.

A self-taught photographer and film maker, Lyon is known for his social documentation during the 1960s and 1970s of those living outside the mainstream of society. Immediately following graduation from the University of Chicago in 1963, he began to chronicle events in the civil-rights movement under the auspices of the Student Nonviolent Coordinating Committee; he later published those photographs in his first book, *The Movement* (1968). Among the countercultures caught by his sympathetic lens are the Chicago Outlaws Motorcycle Club, the street urchins of Santa Marta and Cartagena, Colombia, and the denizens of the Texas prison system, the series in which *The Boss* appears. Always sensitive to the tyrannized, Lyon poses an ironic question in *The Boss*: who, of the two shown here, has the real authority, the rider or the ridden?

123. GARRY WINOGRAND. American, 1928–1984. *Fort Worth, Texas*. 1974. Silver print, 6 × 9". Courtesy Fraenkel Gallery, San Francisco/Estate of Garry Winogrand

The Fort Worth Fat Stock Show and Rodeo is an annual event that was begun in 1896, thirty years after the first herd of Longhorn cattle was driven through the declining village of Fort Worth on its way from South Texas to market in Kansas. The townspeople encouraged the cattle drives, and with the arrival of the railroad, refrigerated railcars, and meat-packing plants, other businesses developed to cater to the cattlemen. The soon-booming town became known as "Cowtown" and "Queen of the Prairies." In 1918, competitive rodeo became Fort Worth's chief form of entertainment. In 1974, the Fort Worth Art Museum commissioned Winogrand to photograph the stock show and rodeo. From the more than a thousand negatives he made between 1974 and 1977, 102 images were selected for publication in his fourth book, *Stock Photographs*. According to Winogrand, his photographic essay was not a journalistic record, but rather a subjective view by someone interested in the physicality and drama of the event.

124. GEOFFREY WINNINGHAM. American, born 1943. *Sandy Wilson, Miss National Appaloosa Queen, With "Jokers Wild" and His Trainer, Houston Livestock Show*. 1972. Silver print, 7½ × 11¼". Courtesy Geoffrey Winningham

The Appaloosa, with its distinctively shaped head, is a pinto-type horse, dappled irregularly with white, black, or brown spots. Evidence of the modern Appaloosa's origins can be found in Ice Age cave paintings of Central Europe and in Greek records of Persian war horses in 480 B.C. Conquering Spaniards brought horses to the New World, and by 1730, a few spotted ones had migrated from Mexico to the northwestern United States. Named for the Palouse River, the Appaloosa breed was systematically developed by the Nez Perce Indians, whose lands occupied the area where Washington, Oregon, and central Idaho converge around the lower Snake River. Recognizing the Appaloosa's sensitivity to handling and easy training, the Nez Perce bred the horse for hunting and pulling heavy loads. Lewis and Clark described the breed as elegant, lofty, and durable in the journal of their 1806 expedition. In his surrender to the white man in 1877, Nez Perce Chief Joseph was forced to relinquish more than a thousand of his precious spotted horses. In later years, Buffalo Bill Cody featured the Appaloosa in his Wild West shows. Winningham's portrait is part of his series on the livestock show and rodeo circuit in Texas.

125. AARON SISKIND. American, 1903–1991. *Old Horse, Chilmark 46*. 1971. Silver print, 9¾ × 9⅝". Courtesy Aaron Siskind/fotomann, inc., New York

An active member of the Photo League, which advocated the application of photography to humanitarian causes, Siskind began his career in 1930 as a social documentarian. In the early 1940s, his work underwent a dramatic change as he abandoned his former style for an abstract, purely pictorial photography that anticipated the work of the Abstract Expressionists. Siskind suppressed the realism of objects in three-dimensional space and created instead a flattened picture plane on which there appeared found and cropped forms and textures—like peeling paint, stone, or graffiti—that would convey symbolic associations. Speaking of his new approach, the photographer said, "The object has entered the picture, in a sense; it has been photographed directly. But it is often unrecognizable; for it has been removed from its usual context, disassociated from its customary neighbors and forced into new relationships" (Lyons, page 24). This image of an old horse dramatically reflects Siskind's abstracting process.

126. RALPH GIBSON. American, born 1939. *Horse's Head and Hand*. 1974. From *Days at Sea* (1975). Silver print, 12¾ × 8¼". Courtesy Ralph Gibson

Gibson began his career in photography in 1962 as an assistant to Dorothea Lange. He moved to New York seven years later, initially to assist Robert Frank on a film. In 1969, he founded Lustrum Press to publish his own work and that of others, notably Frank's *The Lines of My Hand* (1972). *Horse's Head and Hand* is characteristic of Gibson's abstract style, isolating and fragmenting an identifiable object and increasing the grainy texture by enlargement. Three-dimensional objects are reduced to a graphic image of two-dimensional patterns and shapes. Gibson's work has been described as Surrealist; *Horse's Head and Hand* also suggests a mystical inspiration.

127. W. EUGENE SMITH. American, 1918–1978. *Skull in Shadow*. 1947. Silver print, 12½ × 10½". Center for Creative Photography, Tucson/Black Star

W. Eugene Smith, master of the narrative photographic essay, was guided by the philosophy that photojournalism should have a moral purpose and that the photographer and editor must take responsibility for their product. His unrelenting principles often put the volatile photographer at odds with his clients. After his return from photographing in the South Pacific during World War II, Smith resumed a stormy relationship with *Life* magazine, producing about fifty assignments between 1946 and 1952. This shadow abstraction of a horse's skull was part of his first large assignment after the war, in which, for a series featuring the States of the Union, the magazine sent him to New Mexico. According to the script, Smith focused on landscapes, recreation, ranches, Hispanic-American and Indian cultures, and portraits of the leading lights in the area's flourishing artistic communities. The essay, "New Mexico, 1947," contained powerful emblems of the Southwest, but was never published.

128. LEE FRIEDLANDER. American, born 1934. *General Andrew Jackson, Lafayette Park, Washington, D.C.* 1973. Silver print, 11 × 14". Courtesy Laurence Miller Gallery, New York

A native of Washington State, Friedlander began to photograph at the age of fourteen. Soon after arriving in New York in 1956, he became associated with photographers Walker Evans, Robert Frank, Garry Winogrand, and Diane Arbus, with whom he would share a bond in art and life. In 1967, John Szarkowski included Friedlander, Winogrand, and Arbus in his pivotal *New Documents* exhibition at the Museum of Modern Art, calling the young photographers "new documentarians" whose mission was to record their own experiences and perceptions of the world rather than to make traditional documentary photographs for social reform. The image of the monument to Civil War General Andrew Jackson is part of Friedlander's project *The American Monument* (Eakins Press, 1976), a series of photographs culled from several thousand negatives made over more than ten years of traveling throughout the United States. With the irony that pervaded the entire undertaking, Friedlander has portrayed the celebrated general astride his rearing charger, majestically saluting the circling birds, who are probably just about to descend upon their customary perch.

129. RICHARD BENSON. American, born 1943. *Augustus Saint-Gaudens's Memorial to the Massachusetts 54th Regiment*. 1973. Platinum print, 11 × 14". Courtesy Richard Benson

This memorial, located near the State House in Boston, was created in 1884–97 by Augustus Saint-Gaudens and dedicated to the celebrated Northern Black regiment led by Colonel Robert Gould Shaw, son of a prominent abolitionist family. In 1863, the regiment staged an assault on Fort Wagner, a Confederate stronghold guarding the entrance to Charleston harbor. The outcome of the battle favored the rebels, and the 54th lost over half its men, including Colonel Shaw. However, a larger victory was won in terms of the new respect earned for the Black soldier, who had been employed until then chiefly in noncombatant service. This monument represents the "mounted-emperor" school of sculpture, which emphasizes the authority and dignity of a leader by portraying him astride a spirited horse. This photograph was one of several views by Richard Benson published in *Lay This Laurel: An Album on the Saint-Gaudens Memorial on Boston Commons* (New York: Eakins Press, 1973). Benson is known for his exquisite photographs using historical processes, such as platinum and gravure, and for his inventive and handcrafted approach to the modern process of offset printing. Most recently, he has expanded the boundaries of photography by inventing a method of painting with a photographic negative.

130. LINDA CONNOR. American, born 1944. *Spanish Rider, Canyon de Chelly, Arizona*. 1987. Silver contact print on printing-out paper, gold-toned, 8 × 10". Courtesy Linda Connor

Connor began photographing petroglyphs—drawings or carvings on rock made by prehistoric or primitive peoples—about 1976, initially in a small canyon near Prescott, Arizona. Since then she has traveled to other sites, including India. According to the photographer, she was attracted to petroglyphs because of their inherent spirituality: "The marks were ancient, yet they seemed vital in relationship to this very beautiful place. It was that sanctification of a place within nature that I think was particularly moving" (Foerstner). Yet Connor also recognizes the irony in using a factual, mechanical instrument like the camera to record emanations of the soul. The horse is a prominent feature of Native American mythology and rock art. *Spanish Rider* depicts a painted Navajo petroglyph, made about three hundred years ago, after the Spanish had arrived in the Southwest. There is a faintly discernible figure, perhaps a priest or conquistador, on the back of the horse.

131. ELAINE MAYES. American, born 1938. *New York Thruway, Christmas (Pegasus)*. 1972. Silver print, 9⅝ × 6½". Center for Creative Photography, Tucson

The sign with the soaring red horse, designed by Jim Nash in 1933 as a trademark for the Socony-Vacuum Oil Company (now Mobil), has become an icon of capitalism. Carrying the positive associations of speed, "horsepower," and reliability, the memorable symbol enhanced the image of the fuel company. The origins of the flying horse are found in the mythological legend of Pegasus, son of Poseidon and Medusa, born of his mother's blood falling into the sea after she was slain by Perseus. Pegasus flew up to Olympus, where he lived in Zeus's stable and carried thunderbolts, the weapons of his master. Also known as the poet's horse, Pegasus is said to have stamped on the ground and caused a spring of water to gush forth, inspiring anyone who drank from it to compose poetry. With his mortal master, Bellerophon, Pegasus defeated the monster Chimera, the Amazons, and various pirates. In her dreamlike interpretation of the mythical horse, photographer and film maker Elaine Mayes has brought poetry and mystery to the tedium of the New York Thruway.

132. HELEN LEVITT. American, born 1918. Untitled—Chalk Drawings. c. 1942. Silver print, 8 × 5½". Courtesy Laurence Miller Gallery, New York

Born in New York City, Levitt has spent the better part of her career focusing on the more tender aspects of inner-city street life. Her lyrical images of children at play often transcend the squalor of their environment. Levitt's education in photography consisted of studies with Walker Evans and later adaptation to Cartier-Bresson's handheld camera technique. She also made two award-winning films with James Agee. Levitt's image of the chalk horses, undoubtedly scratched on the side of a streetlight by small hands, suggests a modern, ephemeral version of the petroglyph in the Canyon de Chelly recorded by photographer Linda Connor (plate 130). Both are examples of primal individual expression.

133. OLIVIA PARKER. American, born 1941. *Carousel 1*. 1982. Gelatin-silver contact print with selenium toning, 12 × 20". Courtesy Olivia Parker/Brent Sikkema Fine Art, New York

From origins in painting, Parker has become one of the more accomplished still-life photographers of her generation. A passionate collector of objects—from old prints and maps to bones, feathers, and bugs—she makes "arranged photographs," still lifes that are set out on the ground, shot from overhead, and then disassembled. In *Carousel 1*, Parker introduced the shadows of the horses from outside the picture frame in order to activate the space, draw attention to gesture, and offset the shallow depth of field characteristic of the camera she uses. Parker has described her works as "diagrams of the unseeable."

134. SALLY MANN. American, born 1952. *Winter Squash*. 1988. Silver print, 6⅞ × 8¾". Courtesy Sally Mann

Mann's book of photographs *At Twelve* portrays the vulnerable stage in a girl's life between childhood and womanhood. These exquisitely crafted photographs of her own children and their friends, often scantily clad, are carefully composed over time with the aid of notes and preliminary photographic sketches. *Summer Squash* hints at the fascination young girls often have with horses. The background of the image is fantasy-like; the suggestively shaped squashes, chickens, and carousel horse envelop and whirl around the child, immersed in her reverie.

135. EILEEN TOUMANOFF. American, born 1924. *The Horse No. 1*. 1987. Silver print, 3⅜ × 5". Courtesy Kathleen Ewing Gallery, Washington, D.C.

A student of painting, Toumanoff discovered pictorial possibilities in photography through workshops with Lisette Model, Ray Metzker, John Gossage, and Emmet Gowin. She has developed her own distinctive method of appropriation by photographing book illustrations and postcards of historical paintings. She distorts these reproductions by manipulating the light dramatically, cropping through the viewfinder, shooting close up, and making final alterations in the darkroom. Her series on the horse began when she became intrigued by a postcard of a George Stubbs painting that was part of a larger still life she was photographing. With a great reverence for the equine form in the history of art, Toumanoff embarked on a series of images using the works of Stubbs and other animal painters. *The Horse No. 1* is abstracted from the Stubbs work *Hambletonian, Rubbing Down*, painted in 1800 for the horse's owner, Sir Henry Vane Tempest. The photographer has cropped the painting in such a way that the groom, trying to calm the excited and perspiring racehorse, is represented only by the tiny detail of fingertips clutching the horse's mane. Toumanoff conveys equine strength and energy in a photograph that belies its painterly origins.

136. RUTH THORNE-THOMSEN. American, born 1943. *Horses, Illinois*. 1976. From the series Expeditions, 1976–83. Toned silver contact print from paper negative, 3¾ × 4¾". Courtesy Ehlers Caudill Gallery Ltd., Chicago

Using a cigar box with a removable back and a pinhole aperture, Thorne-Thomsen photographs whimsical imaginary landscapes reminiscent of nineteenth-century expeditionary views by Maxime DuCamp or J. B. Greene. Her use of paper negatives and sepia toning further suggests photography's primitive origins. In Thorne-Thomsen's miniature tableaux of toys and cutouts, the horses appear as a galloping blur across the landscape of sand and water and at the same time seem frozen in stone, like ancient monuments mysteriously deposited in a barren landscape. Ambiguities in context, scale, and time confuse the notion of reality and confound expectations of a photographic image.

137. JED DEVINE. American, born 1944. *Toy Horses on Carpet*. 1978. Palladium print, 7½ × 9½". Courtesy Bonni Benrubi Fine Art Photographs, New York

Devine, who studied photography at Yale, began working in palladium in 1977. He was drawn to the process by its inherent warm color, the potentially infinite range of middle tones, and the rich assortment of papers available for printing. Devine's photograph of toys and shells scattered on a carpet conveys a sensuousness that is characteristic of his intricate, dense images. Although it addresses formal concerns of viewpoint, scale, texture, and context, it also suggests a narrative, a mysterious drama played out between the black-and-white horses and their Surrealistic landscape.

138. WILLIE ANNE WRIGHT. American, born 1924. *Civil War Redux: Federal Cavalry, Gettysburg*. 1988. Silver print, 3¾ × 4½". Courtesy Willie Anne Wright

In 1987, Wright discovered the phenomenon of the Civil War reenactment, an authentically staged event begun in the 1960s in which as many as forty thousand participants pose as Confederate and Union soldiers to recreate Civil War battles and events. By 1990, Wright had recorded twelve of these reenactments and assembled a body of work she called *Civil War Redux*. A veteran of the lensless pinhole-camera format, Wright has used this most primitive and poetic of photographic processes to merge two realities, the past and present, into hauntingly evocative images. Exploiting the distorting effects of long exposures and the inherent soft focus and infinite depth of field produced by the pinhole camera, she has created blurred images of timeless dimension. Occasionally, she suggests a time warp by allowing modern objects, such as a pickup truck, to intrude on an otherwise historically accurate image. Views such as this one of the Federal cavalry are modern reminders of the horse's once-central role in war.

139. MICHAEL SPANO. American, born 1949. *City Cowboys, New York City*. 1988. Silver print from eight-frame negative, 50 × 40". Courtesy Laurence Miller Gallery, New York

Spano's work combines the often ordinary subject matter of street photography with the invention and expressiveness of art photography. In the past, Spano has experimented with various cameras and shooting techniques as well as with selective solarization, photograms, panoramas, and varying print sizes. More recently, he has worked with a camera in which eight lenses are automatically triggered three seconds apart by pressing the shutter. The three-second delay allows the photographer to move the camera between each exposure, and the result is a cinematic collage of visual fragments. While Spano's earlier solarizations have been called Surrealistic, these large eight-frame works, composed of different viewpoints within the same overall image, suggest the simultaneity of Cubism. Here, the rural subject, cowboys, on the most urban of streets intensifies the effect of disorientation.

140. ANDY WARHOL. American, 1928–1987. *Horse Behind Gate*. 1976/1986. Four silver prints sewn together, 22 × 28". Courtesy Robert Miller Gallery, New York

Warhol's early work in the 1950s was inspired by photographs from the media depicting stereotypes of popular culture. From the 1960s on, he actually used the photographic process as a partner of painting, in his photo-silkscreens embellished with paint. An inveterate shutter bug, Warhol published several books of his snapshots. *Horse Behind Gate* is from a series made near the end of his life in which he had sewn together four identical black-and-white photographs of various subjects. Although this work is purely photographic, it is also reminiscent of his multiple portrait paintings and of the Minimalist grid motif in American painting and sculpture during the 1960s and 1970s.

141. SYLVIA PLACHY. Hungarian, born 1943. *Night Mare*. 1980. Silver print, 5 × 7⅜". Courtesy Sylvia Plachy

Born in Hungary, photojournalist Sylvia Plachy has been a free-lance photographer in New York City since 1965. Although her work has appeared in national and international publications, she is perhaps best known for her regular contributions to New York's *Village Voice*, for which she has been a staff photographer since 1978. Plachy's photographs combine the disconcerting realities of Diane Arbus's imagery with the poetic lyricism of André Kertész, her compatriot and mentor. In *Night Mare*, the effort and strength of the animal, thrashing with teeth bared and nostrils flaring through the water, are almost palpable; the image graphically illustrates the pun in its title.

142. ALEKSANDRAS MACIJAUSKAS. Lithuanian, born 1938. *In the Veterinary Clinic*. 1978. Silver print, 6⅜ × 9½". Courtesy Aleksandras Macijauskas

Macijauskas is at the forefront of a group of Baltic photographers who are using the medium as a social tool in the struggle for national identity and the right to self-determination. A member of the Society of Creative Photography of the Lithuanian Soviet Socialist Republic, established in 1969, Macijauskas tends toward realism rather than romanticism, irony rather than optimism. He characteristically uses the photographic process itself to intensify the emotional drama in his images. In his series on a veterinary clinic, he has at various times used a wide-angle lens, a distorted spatial perspective, blurring, and lens reflection in his representation of frightened and isolated animals. The images often suggest metaphors for the plight of the individual in Macijauskas's homeland.

143. RICHARD MISRACH. American, born 1949. *Dead Animals No. 79*. 1987. From the series Desert Cantos VI/The Pit, 1987–88. Ektacolor Plus print, 40 × 50". Courtesy Richard Misrach/fotomann, inc., New York

The northern Nevada desert is littered with the carcasses of horses who have died as a result of grazing on land believed to be contaminated with plutonium from secret nuclear tests conducted by the United States government during the 1950s. In a multipart work representing the devastating effects of man's use and misuse of the American desert, Misrach has photographed roadways, military bases, flood areas, desert fires, bombing ranges, and dead-animal pits. Using his art in the service of politics and the environment, he has created an image that is both horrifying and disarmingly beautiful. Misrach refers to this series of photographs as "latter-day *Guernicas*."

144. RICHARD H. ROSS. American, born 1947. *Deyrolle Taxidermy, Paris, France*. 1985. Ektacolor Plus print, 30 × 30". Courtesy Richard H. Ross

Since 1977, Ross has been photographing dioramas in natural-history museums throughout the world, in a body of work he calls his Museology series. Born in Brooklyn, Ross first encountered dioramas as a child; his interest was nurtured at the American Museum of Natural History in Manhattan, where he gazed on masterpieces of taxidermy placed in painterly environments. In the early 1980s, he discovered the musty rooms of the Musée National d'Histoire Naturelle in Paris and began to record their haunting, silent displays of stuffed animals—some freestanding in the dark halls, some in glass cases, some huddled together in storage, all in various stages of disintegration from lack of care. Ross's work also takes him directly to taxidermists such as this Parisian establishment that houses a large horse living incongruously in cluttered harmony with animals from all sorts of exotic habitats.

145. JAN GROOVER. American, born 1943. Untitled (Angel and Horse Atop Column). 1987. Type C print, 16¼ × 18½". Courtesy Robert Miller Gallery, New York

Trained as a painter, Groover became attracted to the photography being used in the Minimal and Conceptual art of the 1970s. Her work evolved from early Minimal color triptychs, through sensual color still lifes of kitchen utensils and plants in the late 1970s, to elegant platinum and palladium still lifes reminiscent of the painter Giorgio Morandi in the early 1980s. In recent years, Grover has returned to color to create dreamlike, painterly photographs of assemblages such as this untitled work, which suggests the mystery of a deserted De Chirico landscape punctuated with classical references. While avoiding manipulation of the print in the darkroom, she does experiment with conventional perspective and shoots with a shallow depth of field, which often gives the background for her objects a strange, undefined glow. Groover has always suppressed narrative interpretations of her photographs, emphasizing instead her concern with form. For her, this curiously dynamic image of the horse and angel is simply what it depicts.

146. JOEL MEYEROWITZ. American, born 1938. *Spain*. 1967. Dye transfer print, 15½ × 23½". Courtesy James Danziger Gallery, New York

Meyerowitz abandoned a career in painting and medical illustration and turned to photography after the experience of accompanying Robert Frank on assignment in 1963. Meyerowitz's painterly origins have continued to influence his work, especially in the sensual use of light in his color photography. He has memorialized the luminosity of Cape Cod in photographs that are reminiscent of Edward Hopper's paintings. Meyerowitz uses color to evoke feeling, whether he is exploring with subtle hues the romanticism of a vast seascape at dusk or using the vibrance of color to describe a confrontation on a street in New York City. His poignant image of the fallen horse in Spain is made more excruciating by the intensity of color and light.

147. DOUG AND MIKE STARN. American, born 1961. *Horses*. 1985–86. Toned silver print, tape, 14 × 24". Courtesy Stux Gallery, New York

A number of contemporary artists have made the image of the horse the subject of their work. In the paintings of Susan Rothenberg or the sculptures of Deborah Butterfield, for instance, the equine form is a vehicle of personal expression. Similarly, one of the photographic projects that brought Doug and Mike Starn to public attention in the mid-1980s was their monumental series of more than a hundred variations on one negative showing a pair of horses' heads. By tearing, taping, folding, scoring, toning, and using other idiosyncratic techniques in the darkroom, the Starns have created photocollages that are often on the scale of contemporary paintings. Their series of horses, completed in three weeks, served as a fundraiser for the Institute of Contemporary Arts in Boston. According to the Starns, the horse sequence is "a dictionary of what we do to an image." It also reflects the identical twins' interest in mirror imagery and numerology.

148. BARBARA NORFLEET. American, born 1926. *Tisbury Great Pond*. 1985. Cibachrome print, 16 × 20". Courtesy Barbara Norfleet

A student of psychology and social relations, Norfleet has had a long affiliation with Harvard University as curator, teacher, and photographer. *Tisbury Great Pond* is part of her most recent series of photographs known as Manscape With Beasts. Norfleet's work has been associated with the contemporary photographic movement called the New Topographics, which investigates the human being's impact on the environment, whether in the form of pollution, acid rain, deforestation of rain forests, or, in Norfleet's case, interactions with other animals who share the earth. Using her own method of street photography, Norfleet lies in wait for hours, ready to capture on film animals wandering into a "manscape," a human environment furnished with human artifacts. Her subjects include a skunk in a campsite, a raccoon near a trash bin, horses peering curiously into a car. The moment of confrontation with the animal is frozen by the light of an electronic flash.

149. HOLLY ROBERTS. American, born 1951. *Frisian Stallion*. 1981. Oil on silver print, 11 × 14". Courtesy Etherton/Stern Gallery, Tucson

Although Roberts is best known as a photographer, she considers herself primarily a painter. A student of printmaking and former curator at the lithography workshop of the Tamarind Institute, she began combining photography with painting toward the end of the 1970s. Starting with a black-and-white photograph as a foundation, Roberts alters its surface by overpainting so that she all but obscures the first process. The original "reality" is buried beneath layers of expressive brushstrokes. Roberts's early work, of which *Frisian Stallion* is an example, used the image of the horse repeatedly as a point of departure. A native of the Southwest and an accomplished rider, she photographed at horse shows, rodeos, parades, and stock shows, gathering source material for later manipulation and distortion with paint.

150. DAVID LEVINTHAL. American, born 1949. Untitled. 1989. From the series Cowboys and Western Landscapes, 1989. Color ink-jet process on canvas, 72 × 72". Courtesy Laurence Miller Gallery, New York

Levinthal is one of a group of contemporary American photographers using toys as surrogates for reality. However, unlike Ruth Thorne-Thomsen (plate 136) or Jed Devine (plate 137), Levinthal has been exploring masculine American myths like the cowboys and Indians of the Wild West. In his narratives, toys and background scenes are fuzzy, and scale is concealed; the entire photograph is often infused with a warm golden light that both alludes to the romantic aura of the West and increases the ambiguity. The stereotypical poses of the cowboys and Indians suggest television and movies as an inspiration. This depiction of a rearing horse—a classic Levinthal image—is also an example of the expanding boundaries of photographic technology. It was created by scanning the original transparency into a computer system which then drove the airbrush guns that reproduced the image on canvas.

151. BETTY HAHN. American, born 1940. *A Starry Night*. 1975. Cyanotype with watercolor and applied silver stars, 22 × 18". Courtesy Andrew Smith Gallery, Santa Fe

The Great Train Robbery of 1903 is considered to be the first Western movie, and William S. Hart was the first Western actor to give his horse, Fritz, equal star status. Following Tom Mix, who was not identified with any one horse, the Lone Ranger appeared with his white stallion, Silver. Silver became part of the Lone Ranger's rallying cry as he and Tonto rode out to restore justice to the land. They joined Gene Autry and Champion and Roy Rogers and Trigger in creating a whole new cult of personality for these trusty equine partners of law and order. In fact, the need eventually arose for "ringing," finding doubles to perform hazardous stunts or to succeed injured, aging, or dead star horses. Photographer Betty Hahn has appropriated the image of the Lone Ranger and Tonto, now a Pop icon, as a vehicle for her experimentation with the boundaries of the photographic medium.

152. RICHARD PRINCE. American, born 1949. Untitled—Cowboys. 1986. Ektacolor print, 27 × 40". Courtesy Barbara Gladstone Gallery, New York

For over a decade, Prince has been rephotographing details from advertisements and presenting them cropped and enlarged, minus their text, in the context of framed and exhibited art. Choosing to defy the traditional concepts of creation, self-expression, and evidence of the artist's hand, Prince appropriates images by "anonymous" advertising photographers. His large, glossy photographs represent the seductive, fictionalized realities used to market products in the world of the mass media. From 1980 to 1986, he produced a series of photographs called Cowboys. In rephotographing cowboy images from the famous Marlboro cigarette ads, Prince reiterates romantic myths and clichés about the cowboy, the West, and the horse. He also suggests how much we accept these myths in our negotiations with modern life.

SELECTED BIBLIOGRAPHY

ABOUT THE HORSE

Barclay, Harold B. *The Role of the Horse in Man's Culture.* London and New York: J. A. Allen, 1980.

Brady, Irene. *America's Horses and Ponies.* Boston: Houghton Mifflin, 1969.

Braider, Donald. *The Life, History, and Magic of the Horse.* New York: Grosset & Dunlap, 1973.

Clark, Kenneth. *Animals and Men: Their Relationship as Reflected in Western Art From Prehistory to the Present Day.* New York: William Morrow, 1977.

Daniels, LeRoy Judson, as told to Helen S. Herrick. *Tales of an Old Horsetrader.* Iowa City: University of Iowa Press, 1987.

Darnley-Smith, Jan. *Horses.* Executive Producer, Russell Galbraith. Scottish Television, 1987.

Dent, Anthony Austen. *The Horse: Through Fifty Centuries of Civilization.* London: Phaidon, 1974.

Dinger, Charlotte. *Art of the Carousel.* Green Village, N.J.: Carousel Art, 1984.

Drager, Marvin. *The Most Glorious Crown.* New York: Winchester Press, 1975.

Drago, Harry Sinclair. *Road Agents and Train Robbers.* New York: Dodd, Mead, 1973.

Durant, John and Alice. *Pictorial History of the American Circus.* New York: A. S. Barnes, 1957.

Evans, Edna Hoffman. *Famous Horses and Their People.* Brattleboro, Vt.: Stephen Green Press, 1975.

Grimshaw, Anne. *The Horse: A Bibliography of British Books, 1851–1976.* London: Library Association, 1982.

Hamilton, Edith. *Mythology.* New York: Mentor Books, 1966.

Jankovich, Miklos. *They Rode Into Europe.* London: George G. Harrap, 1971.

Lawrence, Elizabeth Atwood. *His Very Silence Speaks: Comanche— The Horse Who Survived Custer's Last Stand.* Detroit: Wayne State University Press, 1989.

———. *Hoofbeats and Society: Studies of Human-Horse Interactions.* Bloomington: Indiana University Press, 1985.

———. *Rodeo: An Anthropologist Looks at the Wild and the Tame.* Knoxville: University of Tennessee Press, 1982.

MacGregor-Morris, Pamela. *The Book of the Horse.* New York: Exeter, 1986.

Richardson, Bill and Dona. *The Appaloosa.* South Brunswick, N.J., and New York: A. S. Barnes, 1972.

St. Leon, Mark. "Miss May Wirth." *Bandwagon,* May/June 1990, pp. 4–13.

Vernam, Glenn R. *Man on Horseback.* New York: Harper & Row, 1964.

See also the sources cited in the notes to Elizabeth Atwood Lawrence's essay, pages 16–17.

ABOUT PHOTOGRAPHY

After Daguerre: Masterworks of French Photography (1848–1900) From the Bibliothèque Nationale. Text by Jean Seguin and Weston J. Naef. Catalogue by Bernard Marbot. New York: Metropolitan Museum of Art, 1981.

Alinder, James, ed. *Wright Morris: Photographs and Words.* Carmel, Calif.: Friends of Photography, 1982.

Apraxine, Pierre. *Photographs From the Collection of the Gilman Paper Company.* Yulee, Fla.: White Oak Press, 1985.

The Art of Photography, 1839–1989. Mike Weaver, ed. New Haven and London: Yale University Press, 1989.

Barrett, Nancy C. *Ilse Bing: Three Decades of Photography.* New Orleans: New Orleans Museum of Art, 1985.

Beaton, Cecil, and Buckland, Gail. *The Magic Image: The Genius of Photography From 1839 to the Present Day.* Boston and Toronto: Little, Brown, 1975.

Bonetti, David. "Rising Starns." *The Boston Phoenix,* Oct. 30, 1987.

Bonnot, Agnès. *Chevaux Photographies.* Paris: Hazan, 1985.

Borcoman, James. *Charles Nègre, 1820–1880.* Ottawa: National Gallery of Canada, 1976.

Braive, Michel. *The Photograph: A Social History.* London: Thames & Hudson, 1966.

Brandt, Bill. *Bill Brandt: Shadow of Light.* New York: Da Capo Press, 1966.

Brassaï. Introductory essay by Lawrence Durrell. New York: Museum of Modern Art, 1968.

Brassaï. *The Secret Paris of the 30's.* New York: Pantheon, 1976.

Brehm, Frederick. Obituary. *Rochester Democrat and Chronicle,* April 5, 1950.

Brown, Mark H., and Felton, W. R. *Before Barbed Wire: L. A. Huffman, Photographer on Horseback.* New York: Bramhall House, 1956.

Bry, Doris. *Alfred Stieglitz.* Washington, D.C.: National Gallery of Art, 1958.

Buckland, Gail. *Fox Talbot and the Invention of Photography.* Boston: Godine, 1980.

Calhoun, Catherine. "Pictures Perfect [Michael Spano]." *New York Press,* May 12, 1989.

Capa, Robert. *Death in the Making.* New York: Covici-Friede, 1938.

Catalogue of the International Exhibition of Pictorial Photography. Buffalo, N.Y.: Albright Art Gallery, 1910.

Chevrier, Jean-François. "Jan Groover: Intérieurs Métaphysiques." *Galeries Magazine,* March 1989.

Coke, Van Deren. *Avantgarde Photography in Germany, 1919–1939.* San Francisco: San Francisco Museum of Art, 1980.

Current, Karen, and Current, William R. *Photography and the Old West.* New York and Fort Worth: Abrams and Amon Carter Museum of Western Art, 1978.

Ducrot, Nicholas, ed. *André Kertész, Sixty Years of Photography, 1912–1972.* New York: Grossman, 1972.

Edwards, Gary. *International Guide to Nineteenth-Century Photographers and Their Works.* Boston: G. K. Hall, 1988.

Edwards, Owen. "Hiro." *American Photographer,* vol. VIII, no. 1 (Jan. 1982), pp. 36–54.

Walker Evans. Introduction by John Szarkowski. New York: Museum of Modern Art, 1971.

Evans, Walker. *American Photographs.* Afterword by Lincoln Kirstein. New York: Museum of Modern Art, 1938.

Ewing, Kathleen. A. *Aubrey Bodine, Baltimore Pictorialist, 1906–1970.* Baltimore: Johns Hopkins University Press, 1985.

Fishwick, Marshall. *General Lee's Photographer: The Life and Work of Michael Miley.* Chapel Hill, N.C.: University of North Carolina Press for Virginia Historical Society, 1954.

Foerstner, Abigail. "Spiritual Terrain—Linda Connor Uses Her Camera to Unlock the Soul." *Chicago Tribune,* Aug. 12, 1990, sec. 6, p. 3.

Fontanella, Lee. *Photography in Spain in the Nineteenth Century.* Dallas: Delahunty Gallery, and San Francisco: Fraenkel Gallery, 1984.

Frank, Robert. *The Lines of My Hand.* Los Angeles: Lustrum Press, 1972.

Frassanito, William A. *Antietam: The Photographic Legacy of America's Bloodiest Day.* New York: Scribner's, 1978.

Friedlander, Lee. *The American Monument.* Essay by Leslie George Katz. New York: Eakins Press Foundation, 1976.

Galassi, Peter. *Henri Cartier-Bresson: The Early Work.* New York: Museum of Modern Art, 1987.

Gardner's Photographic Sketch Book of the Civil War. New York: Dover, 1959.

Gelman, Judith. "It's a Wide, Wide, Widelux World, Michael Spano." *Modern Photography,* Oct. 1987, pp. 56–57.

Gernsheim, Helmut and Alison. *The History of Photography, 1685–1914.* New York: McGraw-Hill, 1969.

Giuliano, Charles. "Diagrams of the Unseeable: At Home with Olivia Parker." *Center Quarterly* [Woodstock, N.Y.: Center for Photography at Woodstock], vol. 11, no. 3 (1990), pp. 8–12.

Grad, Bonnie L., and Riggs, Timothy A. *Visions of City and Country, Prints and Photographs of Nineteenth Century France.* Worcester, Mass.: Worcester Art Museum, and New York: American Federation of Arts, 1982.

Green, Jonathan. *American Photography, A Critical History, 1945 to the Present.* New York: Abrams, 1984.

Greenough, Sarah, and Hamilton, Juan. *Alfred Stieglitz: Photographs and Writings.* Washington, D.C., and New York: National Gallery of Art and Callaway Editions, 1983.

Grundberg, Andy. "A Pair of Shows for a Pair of Trendy Twins." *The New York Times,* Oct. 2, 1988.

———. "Taming Unruly Reality." *The New York Times,* March 15, 1987.

Hambourg, Maria Morris, and Phillips, Christopher. *The New Vision: Photography Between the World Wars.* New York: Metropolitan Museum of Art and Abrams, 1989.

Hambourg, Maria Morris, and Szarkowski, John. *The Work of Atget: The Art of Old Paris.* New York: Museum of Modern Art, 1982.

The Hampton Album. Essays by Lincoln Kirstein. New York: Museum of Modern Art, 1966.

Haworth-Booth, Mark, ed. *The Golden Age of British Photography, 1839–1900.* Millerton, N.Y.: Aperture, 1984.

Homer, William I. *Alfred Stieglitz and the Photo-Secession.* Boston: Little, Brown, 1983.

Howe, Graham, and Hawkins, G. Ray, eds. *Paul Outerbridge, Jr.: Photographs.* New York: Rizzoli, 1980.

Jacobs, Joseph. "The Starn Twins." *Splash,* Nov./Dec. 1987, unpaginated.

Jammes, André, and Janis, Eugenia Parry. *The Art of the French Calotype, With a Critical Dictionary of Photographers, 1845–1870.* Princeton, N.J.: Princeton University Press, 1983.

Jareckie, Stephen B. *Photographs of the Weimar Republic*. Worcester, Mass.: Worcester Art Museum, 1986.

Johnson, William S., ed. *W. Eugene Smith: Master of the Photographic Essay*. Millerton, N.Y.: Aperture, 1981.

Jussim, Estelle. *Stopping Time: The Photographs of Harold Edgerton*. New York: Abrams, 1987.

Knight, Christopher. "Photographer Levinthal Goes 'West.'" *Los Angeles Herald Examiner*, April 14, 1989, p. 4.

Koudelka, Josef. *Exiles*. New York: Aperture, 1988.

———. *Gypsies*. Millerton, N.Y.: Aperture, 1975.

Kraus, Hans P., Jr., and Schaaf, Larry J. *Sun Pictures: Llewelyn, Maskelyne, Talbot, A Family Circle*. New York: Hans P. Kraus, Jr., n.d.

Dorothea Lange. Essay by Christopher Cox. New York: Aperture, 1987.

Lemann, Nicholas. *Out of the Forties*. New York: Simon & Schuster, 1983.

Liebling, Jerome. Letter to authors, Nov. 1, 1990.

———. *Jerome Liebling: Photographs*. Amherst, Mass.: University of Massachusetts Press, 1982.

Link, O. Winston. *Steam, Steel, and Stars: America's Last Steam Railroad*. New York: Abrams, 1987.

Lyons, Nathan, ed. *Aaron Siskind: Photographer*. Rochester, N.Y.: George Eastman House, 1965.

Manchester, William; Lacouture, Jean; and Ritchin, Fred. *In Our Time: The World as Seen by Magnum Photographers*. New York: American Federation of Arts in association with Norton, 1989.

Mann, Sally. *At Twelve*. New York: Aperture, 1988.

Martin, Rupert, ed. *Night Trick by O. Winston Link: Photographs of The Norfolk & Western Railway, 1955–60*. London: Photographers' Gallery, 1983.

Meltzer, Milton. *Dorothea Lange, A Photographer's Life*. New York: Farrar Straus Giroux, 1978.

Meredith, Roy. *Mathew Brady's Portrait of an Era*. New York and London: Norton, 1982.

Miller, Francis Trevelyan, ed. *The Photographic History of the Civil War in Ten Volumes*. Vol. 4. New York: Francis Trevelyan Miller, 1911.

Moolman, Valerie. "Alen MacWeeney: An Irish Odyssey, The Tale of the Tinker." *Aperture*, no. 82 (1979), pp. 54–65.

Wright Morris: Photographs and Words. Carmel, Calif.: Friends of Photography, 1982.

Muchnic, Suzanne. "On Safari Amid Dusty Dioramas [Richard Ross]." *Los Angeles Times*, March 20, 1983.

Naef, Weston J. *The Collection of Alfred Stieglitz: Fifty Pioneers of Modern Photography*. New York: Metropolitan Museum of Art, 1978.

Naef, Weston J., and Wood, James N. *Era of Exploration: The Rise of Landscape Photography in the American West, 1860–1885*. Buffalo, N.Y.: Albright-Knox Art Gallery, and New York: Metropolitan Museum of Art, 1975.

Newhall, Beaumont. *The Daguerreotype in America*. 3rd rev. ed. New York: Dover, 1976.

———. *The History of Photography*. Rev. ed. New York: Museum of Modern Art, 1982.

Newhall, Nancy. *P. H. Emerson*. Millerton, N.Y.: Aperture, 1975.

Noble, Alexandra. *The Animal in Photography: 1843–1985*. London: Photographer's Gallery, 1985.

Norfleet, Barbara. *Manscape With Beasts*. New York: Abrams, 1990.

Norman, Dorothy. *Alfred Stieglitz: Introduction to an American Seer*. New York: Duell, Sloan and Pearce, 1960.

The North American Indian: Photographs by Edward Curtis. Millerton, N.Y.: Aperture, 1972.

Cas Oorthuys. Essay by Susan Herzig. New York and San Francisco: Photofind Gallery, and Paul M. Hertzmann, 1990.

Ozment, Judith. "Early Equine Photography." *National Sporting Library Newsletter*, no. 20 (June 1985), unpaginated.

Papageorge, Tod. *Walker Evans and Robert Frank: An Essay on Influence*. New Haven: Yale University Art Gallery, 1981.

Peeps, Claire. "Holly Roberts: Spiritualism in the Everyday Outerworld." *Photographic Insight*, journal 1, no. 4 (1989), pp. 21–26.

Perpetual Motif: The Art of Man Ray. Washington, D.C.: Smithsonian Institution, and New York: Abbeville, 1988.

A Personal View: Photography in the Collection of Paul F. Walter. Essay by John Pultz. New York: Museum of Modern Art, 1985.

The Photographs of Frank B. Fiske. Brochure. Bismarck, N.D.: State Historical Society of North Dakota, n.d.

Pitts, Terence. *Photography in the American Grain: Discovering a Native American Aesthetic, 1923–1941*. Tucson: Center for Creative Photography, 1988.

Plachy, Sylvia. *Sylvia Plachy's Unguided Tour*. New York: Aperture, 1990.

Pollack, Peter. *The Picture History of Photography*. New York: Abrams, 1958.

Rand, Carol. "Willie Anne Wright—Civil War Redux." *Art Letter* [Virginia Beach Center for the Arts], vol. 6, no. 2 (April/May 1990), unpaginated.

Renger-Patzsch, Albert. *Die Welt ist schön*. Munich: Einhorn, 1928.

Rian, Jeffrey. "Expressing the Environment. Richard Prince." *Tema Celeste*, Dec. 1987/Feb. 1988, pp. 74–75.

Richardson, Nan, and Hagen, Charles, eds. *Photostroika: New Soviet Photography*. New York: Aperture, 1989.

Rosenblum, Naomi. *A World History of Photography*. New York: Abbeville, 1984.

Rosenblum, Walter and Naomi. *America and Lewis Hine*. Essay by Alan Trachtenberg. Millerton, N.Y.: Aperture, 1977.

Roth, Evelyn. "A Kind of Violence." *American Photographer*, April 1989, p. 28.

Rudisill, Richard. *Mirror Image: The Influence of the Daguerreotype on American Society*. Albuquerque, N.Mex.: University of New Mexico Press, 1971.

Russell's Civil War Photographs. Preface by Joe Buberger and Matthew Isenberg. New York: Dover, 1982.

August Sander: Photographs of an Epoch. Historical Commentary by Robert Kramer. Millerton, N.Y.: Aperture, 1980.

Schwarz, Arturo. *Man Ray: The Rigour of Imagination*. London: Thames & Hudson, 1977.

The Second Empire, 1852–1870: Art in France Under Napoleon III. Notes by Eugenia Parry Janis. Philadelphia: Philadelphia Museum of Art, 1978.

Slemmons, Rod. *Like a One-Eyed Cat: Photographs by Lee Friedlander, 1956–1987*. New York: Abrams, 1989.

Snyder, Joel. *American Frontiers: The Photographs of Timothy O'Sullivan, 1867–1874*. Millerton, N.Y.: Aperture, 1981.

Sobieszek, Robert A. *The New American Pastoral: Landscape Photography in the Age of Questioning*. Rochester, N.Y., and New York: George Eastman House and Whitney Museum of Art, 1990.

Solomon-Godeau, Abigail. "Allusive Illusions: Ruth Thorne-Thomsen's 'Expedition Series.'" *Print Collector's Newsletter*, vol. 15, no. 4, Sept./Oct. 1984, pp. 133–35.

Spangenberg, Kristin L. *Photographic Treasures from the Cincinnati Art Museum*. Cincinnati: Cincinnati Art Museum, 1989.

Steichen, Edward. *A Life in Photography*. New York: Doubleday, 1963.

Strand, Paul. *Paul Strand: A Retrospective Monograph, the Years 1915–1968*. Millerton, N.Y.: Aperture, 1971.

Paul Strand, Sixty Years of Photographs. Profile by Calvin Tomkins. Millerton, N.Y.: Aperture, 1976.

Szarkowski, John. *Irving Penn*. New York: Museum of Modern Art, 1984.

———. *The Photographer's Eye*. New York: Museum of Modern Art, 1966.

———. *Photography Until Now*. New York: Museum of Modern Art, 1989.

Taft, Robert. *Photography and the American Scene: A Social History, 1839–1889*. New York: Dover, 1964.

Thornton, Gene. *Masters of the Camera*. New York: Holt, Rinehart and Winston, 1976.

Travis, David. *Photographs From the Julien Levy Collection, Starting With Atget*. Chicago: Art Institute of Chicago, 1976.

Van Haften, Julia. *Berenice Abbott, Photographer: A Modern Vision*. New York: New York Public Library, 1989.

Weaver, Mike. *Julia Margaret Cameron: 1815–1874*. Boston: Little, Brown, 1984.

———. *Alvin Langdon Coburn: Symbolist Photographer*. New York: Aperture, 1986.

Welling, William. *Photography in America: The Formative Years, 1839–1900*. New York: T. Y. Crowell, 1978.

Weston, Charis Wilson, and Weston, Edward. *California and the West*. New York: Duell, Sloan and Pearce, 1940.

White, Nancy, and Esten, John. *Style in Motion, Munkácsi Photographs '20's, '30's, '40's*. New York: Clarkson N. Potter, 1979.

Winogrand, Garry. *Stock Photographs, The Fort Worth Fat Stock Show and Rodeo*. Austin and London: University of Texas Press, 1980.

Witkin, Lee D., and London, Barbara. *The Photograph Collector's Guide*. Boston: New York Graphic Society, 1979.

CHESTER COLLEGE LIBRARY

ACKNOWLEDGMENTS

The idea for this book originated seven years ago and has lived through periods of intense activity and excitement, unavoidable interruptions, and great lulls. Steve Schoenfelder has remained with us since the beginning and has variously encouraged and calmed us and showed us new solutions. He is far more than a distinguished designer of books; for us, he has been a friend and true partner.

We owe our deepest thanks to the photographers who were so generous in granting permission to reproduce their works and so patient in answering our queries about the photographs. This book, of course, would have been impossible without their support.

We are extremely grateful to the following collectors, curators, archivists, and dealers around the world who assisted us in researching the images, arranging for reproduction permissions, and securing copyprints: Alice Adam; Mary L. Albar, Hiro Studio; James C. Anderson, University of Louisville; Pierre Apraxine and Howard Gilman, Gilman Paper Company; Vi Au, Black Star; Piero Becchetti, Raccolta Fotografica Giuseppe Primoli, Rome; Gordon L. Bennett; Bonni Benrubi; Barbara Benson; James Borcoman, Susan Campbell, and Hazel McKenzie, National Gallery of Canada, Ottawa; Martha Chahroudi, Philadelphia Museum of Art; Evelyn Daitz, The Witkin Gallery, Inc.; James Danziger; Carol Ehlers and Shashi Caudill; Terry Etherton and Sharon Alexandra, Etherton/Stern Gallery; Kathleen Ewing; Michele Falzone del Barbaro; Pamela C. Feld, The Ansel Adams Publishing Rights Trust; Roy Flukinger and Carey Thornton, Harry Ransom Humanities Research Center; Jeffrey Fraenkel, Frish Brandt, and Amanda L. Doenitz; Peter Galassi, Catherine Evans, and Tom Grischkowsky, The Museum of Modern Art, New York; Noëlle Giret and Glenn Myrent, Cinémathèque Française, Paris; Howard Greenburg and Carrie Springer; Kathy Grosset, Rapho; Robert Gurbo, The Estate of André Kertész; Jim Harris and Calvert Brown, Rena Branstein Gallery; G. Ray Hawkins and Ann Kurtz; Françoise Heilbrun, Musée d'Orsay, Paris; Robert Hershkowitz; Susan Herzig and Paul Hertzmann; Therese Heyman and Drew Johnson, The Oakland Museum; Elizabeth Holmes, Buffalo Bill Historical Center; Edwynn Houk; Corrine P. Hudgins, The Museum of the Confederacy, Richmond, Va.; Charles Isaacs; Matthew R. Isenberg; Gus Kayafas, Palm Press, Inc.; Jerry Kearns, Library of Congress; Robert Koch; Hans P. Kraus, Jr.; Ron Kurtz and Helaine Pardo, Commerce Graphics Ltd.; Marcel LeFranc, Agence VU, Paris; Janet Lehr; Cheryl Leibold and Judy Moore, Pennsylvania Academy of Fine Arts, Philadelphia; Keith de Lellis; Gérard Lévy and François LePage; Nancy Lieberman and Julie Saul; Conchita Link; Patricia McCabe, Irving Penn Studio; Peter MacGill; Ezra Mack; Robert Mann; Bernard Marbot, Bibliothèque Nationale, Paris; Alexandra R. Marshall; Amy Martin, Computer Image Systems, Los Angeles; Rolf Mayer; Nancy Medwell; Richard and Ronay Menschel; Larry Miller and Susanna Wenniger; Anthony Montoya, Paul Strand Archive; Josephine Morris; Lory Morrow, Montana Historical Society; Joan Munkacsi; Greg Parkinson, Robert Parkinson, and Bill McCarthy, Circus World Museum; Fred Pernel, National Archives, Washington, D.C.; Christian Peterson, Ted Hartwell, and Melissa M. Moore, The Minneapolis Institute of Arts;

Terence Pitts, Diane Nilson, and Victor La Viola, Center for Creative Photography, Tucson; Jill Quasha; Howard Read, III, Robert Miller Gallery; Ann Rittenberg and Tracy DiSalvo, Julian Bach Literary Agency; Richard Rudisill and Arthur Olivas, Museum of New Mexico; Janet Russek and David Scheinbaum; Gerd Sander; William L. Schaeffer; Charles Schwartz; Brent Sikkema; Ruth Silverman; Andrew Smith; Frederick Sommer; Thomas Southall and Barbara McCandless, Amon Carter Museum; Todd Strand, State Historical Society of North Dakota; Stefan Stux and Ann S. LaCasce, Stux Gallery; Jo C. Tartt; Roger Taylor and Yasmin Whitehouse, National Museum of Photography, Film and Television, Bradford, England; Jay Tobler, Barbara Gladstone Gallery; David Travis and Sylvia Wolf, The Art Institute of Chicago; Stanley Triggs, McCord Museum, Montreal; Tina Tryforos, Magnum Photos, Inc.; Martin Weinstein; Carlton Willers; David Wooters, Pat Musoff, Janice Madhu, and the late Caralee Aber, George Eastman House.

Throughout this undertaking, we have been inspired by the writings of Elizabeth Atwood Lawrence. We feel very fortunate that she has contributed her insights to our book.

For their encouragement and enthusiasm in anticipation of the forthcoming exhibition of these photographs, we thank Kahren Jones Arbitman, Director, Randy J. Ploog, and Charles Garoian, The Palmer Museum of Art at The Pennsylvania State University. Those at the School of Visual Arts at Penn State have been especially helpful, and we extend our profound thanks to James Stephenson, Director, Kitty Haupt, Darlene Mader, and Marc Hessel. We owe a great debt in particular to Holly Ping, who has been more than generous with her time and patience in helping us to contact lenders and copyright holders; our work would have been next to impossible without her. We extend our appreciation to Penn State's Institute for the Arts and Humanistic Studies and College of Arts and Architecture Faculty Research program, from which we received partial research funds in the initial stages of this project.

Margaret Donovan, our editor at Harry N. Abrams, Inc., listened and lent her encouragement to our proposal seven years ago. Her interest endured, and she has guided two neophytes through the publishing process with great understanding. She has exceeded her duties as a superb editor. We are very grateful to Sam Antupit, director of art and design at Abrams, who has graciously worked with our designer, Steve Schoenfelder, and provided us with gentle guidance. Finally, our thanks to Paul Gottlieb, president and publisher at Abrams, for saying yes.

Over the long period of this project, there have been many colleagues and friends who have exchanged ideas with us and lent their support. We beg forgiveness of those overlooked and cite the following, who have been there when special help was needed: Pierre Apraxine, Jan Brodie, Sherry DeLeon, Aida and Bob Mates, Cusie Pfeifer, and Judy Smilow. Our special thanks to Judy and Paul Corlett for bringing us together; the passion we all shared for horses and photography provided the seed of this idea.

We thank our families for their interest, support, and love. To our spouses, Jennifer and John, we dedicate this book.

INDEX OF PHOTOGRAPHERS

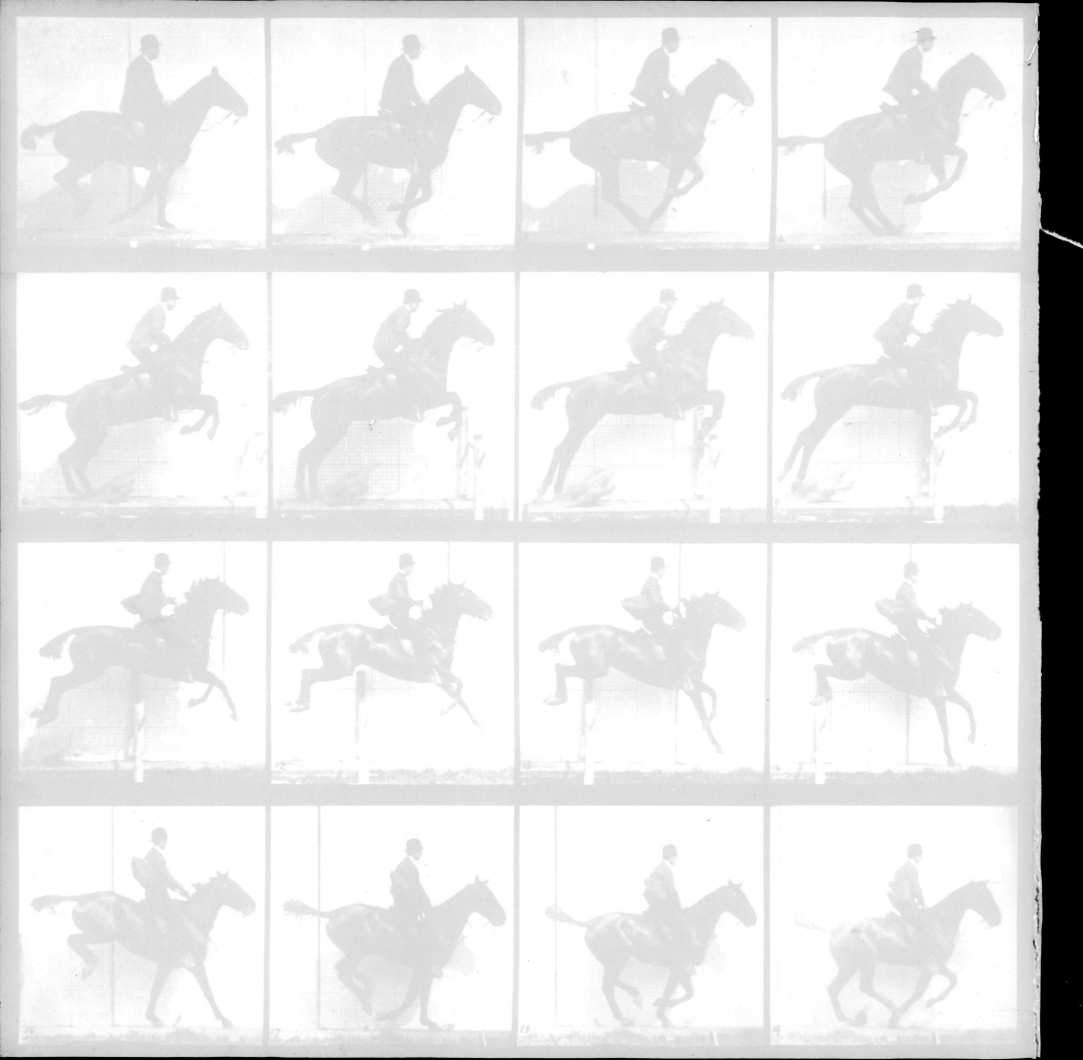